No More Drama

A Practical Guide to Healthy Relationships

Gregory J. Boyce M.A.

Soul Dance Query
Guelph ON Canada

www.NoMoreDrama.ca

ISBN: 978-0-9878135-0-3

Table of Contents

Appreciations

This is quite a dance, being a human being, isn't it?

The music of life is constantly changing. My assessment is that how well I flow to it has significant influence on my enjoyment of it. Having partners that flow in harmony with me is a blessing.

So, here follows a list of sweet partners for the writing of this book...

My review board: Your comments, suggestions, and most of all your strokes were like bubbles of energy. Many thanks to Aggie, Anne, Brenda, Cindy, Errol, Greg, Jen, Joan, John, Julia, Liz, Madeline, Matt, Rosanna, Michael, Ross, Adrienne, Bruce, and Jacob. Special thanks to James, Tammy, Robin, and Gale for your timely & loving encouragement!

My mentors: Your Long standing invitations for me to look for, believe in, and develop who I could be, were pivotal to this writing. Deep thanks to you Karen Davis, Clark Reed, Nancy Wardle, Laurel Thom, Vann Joines, Heidi McBratney, Wake and Kinlen Wheeler.

I am grateful to the Transactional Analysis community for your elucidation of the dynamics of drama. In doing so I think you invited the rest of us to live up to our healthy relationship possibilities.

I've decided to endnote specific references to original works so that readers who are interested in the historical development of the material presented can investigate further. And with that intention, if you, as a reader find something that you'd like me to reference in the next revision, please contact me.

I am most appreciative to you my wife Barbara. When I see you smile at me, when I feel your hand on my shoulder as I type, when I listen to your thoughtful suggestions about a paragraph I've sweated over, I giggle inside with joy because I'm thinking you love me. What a dance partner you are!

Sept.12 2011

Foreward by Clark S. Reed, M.Div., TSTA

It is a daunting task for me to write just a *few* lines for Greg's work about 'drama' because the author shifts the emphasis from Eric Berne's 'games' to 'drama' and makes the focal point 'the drama triangle,' which Steve Karpman is purported to have sketched at an NFL football game years ago.

I like this shift as for me it makes increasing awareness of 'faces' (a word which Greg uses) simple and understandable.

Having said the above, in addition to re-awakening interest in viewing these painful, predictable sequences in a simple geometric figure (a triangle) I find Greg's subsequent six chapters making an important contribution to the body of knowledge: by defining intimacy in a creative way as being hopeful and profound; by giving specific useful examples of how to transact to avoid drama (Living in a Drama Free Zone); sharing the trio of behaviors to eliminate for a drama free life (stop discounting, make clear contracts, and ask for what we want in a clear understandable way); a summary section in each chapter that makes review easy and understandable; and positing in his final chapter where living a drama free life eventuates in a special calm loving death.

The alternative to drama according to Greg is intimacy.

His definition: Intimacy is the capacity to relate to another person in an honest emotionally open equal and caring way that includes transparency, vulnerability and reciprocity. I believe Greg has a point here. Intimacy is the only way to structure time that makes a drama free life desirable.

Some theorists in the past have doubted that it could be achieved. This is an important point Greg is proposing and makes the read important if it were the only point. There are more important points however.

Gregory's final chapter, A Dramatic Finish portrays importantly how the outcome of getting unhooked from the 'addiction' to drama (my term) provides the opportunity to develop skills and ability to choose a calm peaceful ending that is beautiful and victorious. His question, 'How do you want to live in your final days as a human?' resonates with me and his invitation to take 100% responsibility for how you live every moment is the necessary prescribed elixir.

Thank you Gregory.

Why do people create so much drama in their lives?

Some of the answers are: It is exciting. It gets us attention. It prevents boredom. It makes life interesting. It structures our time. It confirms certain beliefs we have about ourselves, others, and the world.

Freud pointed out that it is a way of attempting to undo something that has been upsetting in our life by replaying it over and over again in the hope of having it turn out differently the next time. The only problem is that it often creates pain, and is a way of sabotaging ourselves from experiencing the happiness we desire.

In this book, Greg Boyce offers us some interesting alternatives to a life of drama. He boldly entitles it *No More Drama*. He helps us see that pursuing drama is a decision. It is up to us. We can decide instead to live a life free of self-created drama.

Drawing on the work of Eric Berne, M.D., a psychiatrist who created a powerful and effective approach to therapy call 'Transactional Analysis' and Steve Karpman, M.D., another psychiatrist, who was one of Berne's early students and who developed the concept of the 'Drama Triangle', Greg follows in Berne's and Karpman's tradition of a simple, direct, no-nonsense approach to therapy. He shows us how we can take charge of our lives and get out of the drama roles of persecutor, victim, and rescuer, and live authentic, self-directed lives.

Drama is actually a cheap substitute for what is really fulfilling for us as human beings. What we all desire in some part of ourselves is to experience true intimacy - to open ourselves up fully to another human being and to have them open themselves up fully to us as well – to understand and be understood. Because we are often afraid to allow ourselves to be that vulnerable, we settle for drama.

I invite you to follow Greg through the following pages of this intriguing book to learn about the kinds of drama that most of us engage in daily and how we can put a stop to it. By following the many helpful and practical suggestions he offers, we can begin to take charge of our lives and live an exciting and fulfilling life of true joy, drama-free!

Chapter 1

What Does Drama Look Like

Discover the Sights and Sounds

John Demo can hardly wait to get home from work to tell his wife how much the boss has been after him all day.

Poor Johnny.

Jane Demo can hardly wait till hubby John comes home so she can tell him how the kids have been pestering her all day.

Poor Janey.

The Demo children are awaiting the arrival of their father, John, because mother has been threatening them all day, "Just wait till your father comes home. He'll straighten you out."

Oh oh kiddies.

Enter Johnny, greeted by Janey, who immediately reports her plight with the children, venting all her frustration.

Johnny has to help his damsel in distress, and yet feels victimized saying, "Aw brother, now I've got to punish, when I wanted to be taken care of." Angrily John stomps into the kid's room - and lets them have all his frustration.

Jane hears their cries, and enters just in the nick of time to rescue her defenseless children and criticize John for going too far.

Johnny stomps out of the house and goes to the local bar, hoping to find someone to understand him.

If you've ever...

- walked away from a conversation wondering, *what the heck just happened there? or what was that all about?* -- Then this book is for you.
- had someone react or over-react to you in a surprising and illogical way, and wondered, *what got into them?* -- Then this book is for you.
- over-reacted to someone and wondered, what got into me? -- Then this book is for you.

Drama delivers 'bad feelings'. It strains, challenges and sometimes destroys relationships. It can cripple and destroy lives. Drama supports mistaken, dysfunctional and unhealthy beliefs about ourselves, others and the world.

I define drama in chapter two; but know this ...

Drama never solves problems.

If you have Drama in your life that you could do without, then this book is for you.

How about some examples?

These are like interesting rare over-ripe vegetables. I'll lay them out on the table as samples, introductory style, and in coming chapters, I'll dissect them so you understand why they smell, and what you can do to avoid them in the future.

So plug your nose ... here we go[1].

A middle age married couple, Flora and Paul are from the suburbs of a major city. Flora supervises a staff of fifteen at an on-line health food store. Paul works as a logistics dispatcher at a trucking company. Celina, Flora's daughter is a modern teen. The family is always in drama. They have a reputation around the neighborhood; and once a year some uproar erupts out from behind closed doors on display for the world. For the purpose of this book, pretend you have a friendship with them.

Sample 1: You're visiting with your friend Flora at the local coffee shop. Flora begins a conversation:

Flora: "I just don't know what to do about Paul. He's so distracted by work these days that he never spends any time with us. I'm beginning to think he's a workaholic." <Deep sigh> "I'm really worried."

You: "Have you tried talking to him?"

Flora: "Yes, of course, but he won't commit to a time when we can discuss it. He says it's all in my imagination."

You: "Have you tried counseling?"

Flora: "Yea, but the counselor said Paul had to come in as well."

You: "Hmm, I know. Wayne Dyer has a great book" <interrupted>

Flora: "I can't read self-help books; Paul hates them and throws them out."

You: "Yea that's a problem. Well, you can always try the sexy approach?"

Flora: <weeping> "I tried that, but he hardly noticed. I feel worse now. I don't want to talk about this anymore, as if you're the expert anyways."

You: <quietly> "Sorry. I was only trying to help."

You might recognize yourself in this example. Maybe you recognize someone else.

Can you see the drama?

Most people have either given advice, or received it at one time or another; and sometimes, perhaps too often it goes badly. By badly I mean one or both people end up with feelings they don't like. After this kind of interaction, the relationship has some tension in it. Neither person knows what just happened, or how to make sense of it. A series of these types of interactions actually threatens the health of any relationship.

We call this example of drama, 'Yes But'. That's from Flora's point of view since she says, "yes but," after each piece of advice. It's called, 'I Was Only Trying To Help' from your point of view, because at the end of the sequence you feel strangely compelled to defend yourself by saying, "I Was Only Trying To Help."

I'll now flip it around so you can see another side of it. Different genders, same type of drama.

Sample 2: You and your buddy Paul are sipping beers and watching the game Saturday afternoon. It's halftime and you casually start a conversation about your motor bike.

You: "Yea, I was out on the bike last night."

Paul: "Beauty of a night for it."

You: "Woulda bin, I didn't get far."

Paul: "How come?"

You: "Runnin' rough."

Paul: "Dirty gas?"

You: "Na, new gas filter, fresh gas."

Paul: "Fouled plugs?"

You: "Na, swapped em out a week ago."

Paul: "Air filter?"

You: "Changed with the gas filter."

Paul: "Well you probably need new rings, I keep tellin' ya man, get rid o that rice burnin' crotch-rocket and get youself a real ride."

You: "As if you're the expert. Meat head."

Paul: "Woa, easy now, I was just tryin' to help."

So once again, maybe you recognize yourself in this sequence. Maybe you recognize someone else.

Can you see the drama?

The dialogue ends 'badly'. Paul might even get up and leave. Henceforth the subject of motorbike problems will likely be taboo. From Paul's point of view we call this drama, 'I Was Only Trying to Help'. From your point of view we call it, 'Yes But' like the previous sample. We could call this male gender version, 'Na, tried that, didn't work.'

Advice giving is potentially a slippery slope into drama. By the end of the next chapter you'll know why. And by the end of the book you'll know how to avoid it.

Let's do a new sample. More odor. More dramatic.

Sample 3: Flora is already home when Paul comes into the kitchen.

Paul: *<Flops down on the sofa with a groan>*

Flora: "Careful with that sofa. *<pause>* What's wrong with you?"

Paul: "Nothin'."

Flora: "Yea, right, all slumped and goofy face."

Paul: "Messed up afternoon is all."

Flora: "I thought you and what's his name, Mr. Midlife Crisis, were watchin' ball or playing with your bikes?"

Paul: "It's tuning our bikes, not playing with our bikes. He got all pissy at me for no reason. So I split. Missed the end of the game. Left my damn beer over there."

Flora: "Well go back there and get it. We spent good money on that beer. It was the premium stuff too."

Paul: "I'm not crawling back there."

Flora: "Well you're not getting any more this week; we got a tight budget ya know, till someone around here gets some overtime."

Paul: "Nag nag nag."

Flora: "I wouldn't have to nag if you were any kind of real man."

Paul: *<jumps up, strides right into her space>* "Don't push me Flora."

Flora: "Or you'll what, go home to mommy?"

Paul: "Arggg" *<punches the sofa>*

5

Flora: "Sorry, sorry."

Paul: "See what you made me do!" *<storms out of the house>*

Flora: "Paul don't go, please honey I'm sorry I made you mad."

In this sample, the drama from Flora's point of view is called, 'Kick Me', meaning she was intending to get kicked. And from Paul's point of view the drama is called, 'See What You Made Me Do', as in she made him kick her.

The majority of us have some kind of experience with an interchange like this. Either we experienced it first hand, or we've witnessed it. Notice how serious it got; and so quickly. As we get further into understanding drama, you'll see how this one is different from the two previous samples only in its intensity. The 'how it works' is exactly the same.

Let's move on to another sample, a sort of clubhouse sandwich. We'll add a player to make it a threesome; we call this, *triangulation*.

Sample 4: While Flora prepares dinner, Paul is setting the table. Flora's teenage daughter Celina wanders in with iPod jacked headphones blaring a head banger. She leans against the counter facing Paul, her step-dad.

Flora: "Paul will you ask her to shut that noise off. It's giving me a headache."

Paul: *<makes hand gesture indicating he wants step daughter to cut the sound>* "Turn it off please."

Celina: *<makes a face, raising her voice>* "What?"

Paul: *<turning his voice volume up>* "Turn it off!"

Celina: *<makes more of a face and upping her voice into a whine>* "What?"

Flora: *<loudly>* "Oh for cryin' out loud, Paul don't just stand there, do something. She knows I get headaches from that crap."

Paul: *<reaches for the headphones, Celina does too, they have a brief struggle. Celina twists away and in so doing the headphone jack pulls from the iPod, snapping the wire>*

Celina: <headset off> "Mom. Did you see that?"

Flora: "What? I saw you trying to give me a headache."

Celina: "He broke my iPod."

Flora: "What are you talking about?"

Celina: "Look, it's totally messed up."

Flora: "What?" <turning to Paul> "Did you?"

Paul: "That's ridiculous. It was an accident."

Celina: "Yea, right, an accident that happened exactly when you were grabbing it."

Paul: "Well maybe if you didn't play that crap so loud that your mother gets a headache, we wouldn't have tried to get you to turn it down."

Flora: "Paul, what's this we business? I didn't tell you to grab her iPod."

Paul: "You're the one getting the headache."

Celina: "You owe me an iPod." <storms out>

Paul: "Oh screw this noise. I was only trying to help you Flora. I'm goin' for a ride."

Flora: "Feeling guilty? Pick up our beer from Mr. Midlife Crisis while you're out."

Ah the drama of it all. The name we use for this drama from Celina's point of view is, 'Let's You and Him Fight'. From Paul's point of view we call this, 'I Was Only Trying to Help'. And from Flora's point of view we call it, 'Blemish', as in finding fault with the others. Notice that all three people exit the drama with 'bad' feelings.

Although I've used adults in this sample, often the three people include two parents and one or more children, even young ones.

A nasty version is called, 'Corner', where an adult psychologically traps a child in a corner. Another version involves a child, often a teen who plays one parent off against the other on some request such as money: "If you won't give me money for the movies I know dad will! Maybe I'll go live with him."

The dynamics of this last example are the same as the previous ones. You'll learn this in the pages to come. And you'll learn how to keep yourself out of these things.

Let's look at a drama that involves one person. Believe it or not, the dynamics are the same even when only one person is involved.

Sample 5*:* Celina secludes herself in her bedroom. She's reviewing a 'look' her math teacher Ms. Davis gave her during class that afternoon. Using her diary, Celina writes the following:

Princess Log, Stardate 5/4/2010 : 19:45 gmt

AlgaeBra gave me the dirty look again today. The gleaming daggers of hatred flashed across the room, and I just barely had time to raise my shields and deflect the energy towards NerdBoy, who as usual was drawing photon torpedo circuit boards. She hates me, I know it. I can feel it. What have I ever done to her? She marks me harder than the other girls. She never answers my questions. She frowns every time she looks my way. She's so mean. I'm so innocent. That's it! She's jealous. I'm young, she's old. I'm beautiful, she's plain. I have a boyfriend, she's a divorcee. I have a whole wonderful life ahead of me, her life is half gone. Did I mention boobs, I have them and she doesn't. Maybe she's still single because men discover she's a Klingon? Nerdboy might know.

What I invite you to notice about this sample is the drama Celina generates within the solo experience. The complete event is taking place in a mental/emotional space. No other people are necessary for her to have a drama.

By the end of the next chapter, you'll understand how this solo drama is like the other samples. And by the end of the book you'll understand why a solo drama is as disempowering to the person as any two person or multi person drama.

This next sample is a version of what we call, 'Wooden Leg'. In this situation a participant uses an actual disability, or a perceived disability – such as a wooden leg - to start the drama. Wooden Leg is hugely popular; and for readers in the health field, you may be particularly susceptible.

Sample 6: After a quiet and tense dinner together, Celina gets up from the table and starts to leave the kitchen.

Flora: "Where are you going? Take your dishes to the sink. I'm not your slave you know."

Celina: *<puts on a pouty face and returns to the table, then takes her dishes to the sink. She turns to leave the room>*

Flora: "Not so fast young lady. It's your turn to do the dishes."

Celina: "Are you serious?"

Flora: "My name is Flora, not serious; but I mean it, you're washing tonight."

Celina: "Ha ha very funny; aren't you forgetting I have an allergy to latex?"

Flora: "What's that got to do with washing dishes?"

Celina: "Washing dishes – hot water – latex gloves - hives?"

Flora: "Start the water."

Celina: "How can you expect someone with a latex allergy to just go ahead and expose themselves to it."

Flora: "Washing dishes – hot water – bare hands – clean dishes."

Celina: "Hot water makes my hands wrinkle and age. You want me to have old woman's hands? So I have to choose between hives and old woman's hands. You're so mean. You have no sympathy for someone with an allergy."

Flora: "Oh forget it. I'll do it myself, like everything else around here! "

This form of drama is often used by people who get themselves influenced by substances. The phrase you'll hear is something like this: "Ya, I'm not really responsible for that. I was drunk at the time."

One last sample before we move on...

Sample 7: Later that evening, as Flora is quietly reading, Celina approaches.

Celina: "Can I talk to you about something?"

Flora: <*Noticing that Celina seems unusually quiet and polite, perhaps even sad, she sets her book down.*> "Sure honey, what's going on?"

Celina: <*Sits down beside Flora on the sofa, and starts to tear up.*>

Flora: <*Softly*> "What is it? What's wrong?"

Celina: "I wonder if you really care about me."

Flora: <*Feeling a sick twist in her stomach*> "Of course I care about you. Why would you think such a thing?"

Celina: "Well, <*starting to cry*> you were pretty mean after supper."

Flora: <*Feeling apprehensive*> "You mean about the dish washing?"

Celina: "Yes. If you want me to move out so you can be alone with Paul you should just tell me."

Flora: <*Surprised*> "Where did you get that idea."

Celina: <*fully crying*> "It's obvious from how you both treat me."

Flora: "I don't want you to move out. I love you. That's a silly idea."

Celina: <*getting up off the sofa and walking away*> "You just don't understand me."

Flora: "Wait. Stay. Give me a chance to understand."

This sample sounds very different than the others doesn't it? As you'll see, there are common elements that define it as drama; and those commonalities are what will help you avoid this type of situation in your own life. This drama by the way, is a mild version of what's called, 'Do Me Something'; meaning, one person attempts to get another to do something for them. In this sample, the deliverables Celina wants Flora to give her is a feeling of being cared for, or understood – but Celina walks out before actually allowing Flora to even get started.

Chapter Summary

So in this first chapter you've been introduced to the sights and sounds of drama in several versions:

'Yes but' coupled with 'I was only trying to help'. 'Kick me' coupled with 'See what you made me do'.

'Let's you and him fight' coupled with 'I was only trying to help' and 'Blemish'.

'Wooden leg' and lastly 'Do me something.'

I like using the colloquial names at times, but actually it's not necessary to know the names. In the following chapter I describe the common components of drama and you'll understand why the names are just descriptive labels.

Mission Possible[2]

Examine a recent dramatic encounter. Create a two column dialogue chart. Put the transactions in the left column, like I've done with the samples, and keep the right column empty for now. Keep your chart handy for chapters to follow. If you choose to take this mission, subsequent chapter missions will invite you to 'work it through'. If you choose to continue with your real life example in missions to follow, you will increase the probability of reducing drama in your life beyond what reading alone will achieve.

Contracting[3]

Later in the book I discuss ways of staying out of drama. One strategy is the use of clear requests, clear responses, and clear agreements. The latter is called contracting. Contracting decreases the probability of drama; which is why contracts are used in many situations, such as financial dealings – except not in all. As a model, I will state what our contract is and by doing so you the reader and I the writer will not set up any drama between us.

The contract between me Gregory, the author and you, the reader:

I agree to describe drama in a manner I think will convey the most important aspects of it, including how to stay drama free. I state that I think you have the desire and motivation to understand what I write and implement changes in your life to reduce or remove drama if you so choose. I know this about you because you're reading this. You agree to read this with a receptive mind which, like a parachute, works best when open. As you consider how this information applies to you, I invite you to experiment with it to discover firsthand how it reduces the drama in your life.

Chapter 2

What's Your Drama Face

Recognizing a Drama

All drama requires at least two active roles. Many dramas use three active roles. And some dramas have a fourth role, a passive one.

The roles are:

1. Victim (active).
2. Persecutor (active).
3. Rescuer (active).
4. Audience (passive).

Notice that I capitalized them. This is to distinguish these as roles and not actual people. A real person can act out all the roles over the course of a short period of time and cannot therefore be defined as just one; although the person may have a favorite role they play again and again. In the previous chapter's examples, each person acted in one or more of the roles.

And when you experience drama in your life, you too are in one of the three roles.

Choices – Choices

In any life situation you have two fundamental choices as to how you respond: you can choose to employ the power of your problem solving and conscious thinking capabilities; or you can respond knee jerk fashion (subconscious) the way you learned while growing up.

The former will require energy, and probably time. The latter will be comfortable, seem right, and be familiar but it will not include all aspects of you and others involved, or the situation. We call that **discounting** [4].

Discounting is when a person ignores information relevant to a situation.

Similar to its use in retailing where a discount to the price of an item reduces its perceived value, so too *during transactions between people, a discount happens when a person or situation is ignored or minimized. The common characteristic for all three active dramatic roles in any drama is the presence of discounting.*

Here's an example of how this happens...

A friend takes you flying in a single engine aircraft and as you cruise along, without really thinking you state, "I could never learn how to fly, I'm not smart enough."

You've just discounted yourself.

Your pilot friend says, "Well I wasn't going to say anything, but I agree with you. Sorry, you don't have it where it counts."

Your friend has just discounted you.

You have some feeling response to what your friend said. By the time you recover enough to reply, the aircraft is on final approach for landing and the pilot is concentrating intensely, but regardless, you say, "I resent you saying that. What gives you the right to judge me?"

You've just discounted the present situation.

In the above example, the initial discount of yourself is a quick judgment that has no evaluative component such as information gathering on what it takes to fly, what training is required, what do the exams include, who typically passes and fails. Nor have you given any thoughtful assessment of your personal attributes and characteristics compared to the requirements for flying.

Your friend's discount is the same in that he or she didn't really think about your traits in relation to the demands of piloting. Neither of you considered that there are several levels of licensing each with its own set of requirements.

Finally, when you ignore the fact that the most critical and sensitive phase of flight is in progress and the pilot's attention needs to be on landing the aircraft you are discounting the situation.

Generally, whenever you find yourself feeling like a **Victim**, **Persecutor**, or **Rescuer** the odds are you're discounting yourself, someone else, a situation, or some combination of the three. Often there are others doing the same thing, so you all do this dance - the disco (discounting) – as seen in the dramatic exchange of transactions in the first chapter.

Discounts are culture dependent.

What this means is, a discount to one person may not be to another. So, different cultures (and subcultures such as families) define discounts differently.

For example, in one family everyone waits for all members to sit at the dinner table before they begin eating. If a member of that family started eating before the last person sat down, the act would be perceived as premature and a discount.

In contrast, in another family, not eating as soon as the food is served would be perceived as a discount of the food or the cook, as in "eat it while it's hot".

Another example of how discounts are culture specific, consider the usage of the word "sick". In one culture it means something bad as in "you're sick to even think of jumping off that cliff;" whereas in another culture it means something good as in, "hey bro, sick jump."

So in the aircraft example above, the 'flying' culture sets the context for the discounts. If you didn't understand the discounts in that example all it means is you're not a member of the culture that defines those discounts.

Here's one more example of how dependent discount thinking is on the cultural context.

I use this example with clients and I call the subculture the 'Little boobs and dickies group'. Members of this subculture believe that a person is gender handicapped proportionate to the diminishing size of their breasts or penis: little boobs or dicks = less than adequate for the gender. So if you're a member of this subculture, you can discount someone else who is a member by referring to their undersized parts.

In sample drama 5, Celina conducts this discount of her teacher with the line, "did I mention boobs, I have them, she doesn't".

We'll return to discounts later. Let's move on, and get deeper into the roles involved in creating drama. Remember that I capitalize the names of the roles to distinguish them as positions in a drama not actual people.

Victim: Poor Me

The Victim will discount (ignore, or minimize) him or herself.

The Victim considers him or herself to be powerless in the relationship or situation and might even lie about an ability to effect change.

The Victim feels oppressed, helpless, hopeless and often ashamed of that 'fact'.

The Victim will use a variety of communication styles to express his or her victimization: whiney, pouty, complaining, sullen, pessimism, doom and gloom, woe is me, cynical. The outstanding trait is a position of 'I can do nothing about this.'

The Victim will attempt to convince you that they have or had 0% responsibility in the matter of their victimhood. It was out of their control. It just happened. During an exchange, they will push to convince you that they have no or little influence. The position of Victim is one of 'no thinking'.

A person in the Victim role will sound and act very convincingly! Some Victims may convert this psychological Victimhood into a real world victim state and can get themselves into real problems.

An experienced Victim will be very compelling; especially when combined with a malady or incapacity of some kind.

Rescuer: Ah Poor Little Victim, Let Me Help You

A person in the Rescuer role will discount (ignore, or minimize) another person by taking the attitude that the other is hopeless, helpless, unable to solve the problem, and generally assumed to be flawed in some way. Because there are real victims in the world who need real rescuers, this dramatic Rescuer role tends to be more subtle and covert than a Victim.

A Rescuer also believes the other role in drama, the Persecutor, is flawed in some way, such as a character defect (cruel, mean, selfish etc.), thereby *discounting* the Persecutor. So the Rescuer is *discounting* both Victim and Persecutor - which is why Rescuers often get beaten up by both other players and told to keep out of it.

A Rescuer often doesn't want to rescue; but does so out of guilt, thinking things like, *who else will take care of this Victim*. And frequently the Rescuer doesn't expect the rescue to actually succeed, thinking something like, *with such a Victim, a rescue is next to impossible*, or *that kind of person cannot be helped*.

Remember, from the Victim side, he or she doesn't want to be rescued because that would end the drama.

There are many styles of rescuer from Mr. Nice Guy to Ms. Helpful; from Mr. Community to Ms. Volunteer; from Mr. Martyr to Ms. Everyone's Best Friend. In every style the common theme is the Rescuer will attempt to solve the Victim's plight.

A practiced Victim will attempt to convince a Rescuer that the problem is a Rescuer problem. A master Victim will engineer problems to actually become the Rescuer's problems!

If you like to give advice, heads up, you probably like the Rescuer role.

Conduct an assessment: are you discounting the other person, thinking they <u>need</u> to know what you have to say or that it's for their own good?

On the other hand, sometimes we're simply enthusiastic about a topic and want to share that excitement, or share our experience; which may sound like advice or a mini-lecture but does not include the *discount*.

Sometimes, Rescuers want attention, and they get it with a self-disclosure that sounds like advice, or a mini-lecture.

Have you ever discounted someone by preventing their opportunity to speak?

17

Have you held the belief that what you want to say is more important than what they're saying?

The other person may feel annoyed that you're now doing the talking, having grabbed the microphone, so to speak. You may not be rescuing, but you've hijacked the conversation as in, "Listen to me, listen to me." This is a *discount* of their self-disclosure. This ties into the next position.

Persecutor: It's Your Own Fault

The Persecutor will *discount* (ignore, or minimize) another person, or him or herself. He or she will state directly or indirectly that the other person is inadequate, stupid, helpless, hopeless, or worthless.

The Persecutor will use a variety of styles to convey the message: blaming, criticism, accusations, sarcasm, gossip, seduction, conning and trickery, cruel or practical jokes ("Hey can't ya take a little joke?"), temper tantrum, violence, threats, trapping and cornering.

The Persecutor holds the belief that the Victim's problems are most likely because of a flaw or defect in personality, character, mental capability, emotional status, genetic makeup, or spiritual nature.

The Persecutor often thinks that nothing would happen if it weren't for them. The Persecutor thinks that they are responsible for anything 'good' that happens; that they are 200% responsible. In fact, they have to be because the Victim is too useless to contribute anything. People who don't delegate or who micro-manage may like the Persecutor role.

Similar to some Rescuers, a Persecutor often grabs center stage by interrupting another person's speaking and in so doing declares, "What I have to offer is more important than what you have!" This is an overt *discount* of the other, and a covert *discount* of all others who are participating.

Furthermore, it's an invitation for others to jump in as Victims or Rescuers (of the one interrupted); or as wanna-be Persecutors (how dare you interrupt me), in which case the two fight for that role.

Two people fighting for the Persecutor position can generate a lot of drama with overt insults or physical altercation.

Audience: Ohh Ahh, What Will Happen Next?

Although *discounting* is not a characteristic of the Audience role in an active fashion, a person who sits in the audience is participating vicariously with one or more roles being acted out. And that's the fascination for a member of the Audience – the identification of themselves up there on stage. If a person does not identify with a drama position, the drama is simply a sequence of behaviors, hardly even curious.

For example, if a conversational scene in a movie is dialogued in a foreign language without subtitles, you would not be very interested in it.

The role of Audience often has importance for why people initiate and participate in drama. The reason for this moves us into the next chapter, The Reasons You Play; but for now I'll just call it attention.

The active roles get attention from the Audience such as cheers and boos. By giving the drama attention, the Audience is actually encouraging and supporting the drama.

The Drama Triangle

Now that our four positions are described we can place them in relation to each other in a triangular diagram, and I'll call the drama by its relational name The Drama Triangle.

This configuration was first described by Stephen Karpman in 1968[5]. Later, it was named the Karpman Triangle. I've also heard it referred to as the Triangle of Disempowerment.

The **Victim** is in the 'one down' position, we draw that role on the bottom of the triangle – so the figure is resting on its point.

Using the colloquial phrase, 'my right hand man' to describe a helper, we place the **Rescuer** position on the right point of the triangle.

The **Persecutor** role goes on the left hand point, as in the phrase, 'coming out of left field'.

19

The Audience sits around the triangle, as any encouraging Audience sits close to the stage, cheering and booing the action and hoping to see some blood & guts.

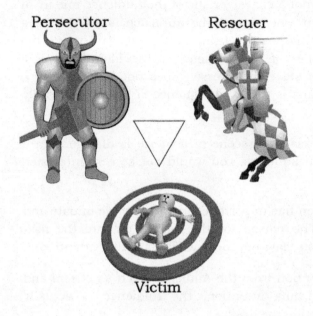

Persecutor   Rescuer

Victim

The Switch (or, the ol switcheroo)

A common and identifying characteristic of the transactions between roles in the drama itself is that at some point, one of the people will switch positions. We'll get into why that is in the next chapter; but for now just know that as the drama continues you can anticipate a switch of roles.

As one person switches, others may switch as well. We say they are 'invited' to switch because it's a choice; an alluring habituated one that has a quality of necessity, but still a choice.

So when you're watching some dramatic transactions, get ready for the switch – it almost always happens. When it does, you know for sure you've just seen the drama triangle in action, and you're in the Audience position.

If you sense that you're in a Victim, Persecutor, or Rescuer role, get ready, brace yourself, because either you or another person on the triangle with you is preparing to switch.

A switch involves moving from a current role to one of the others.

For example, if you started in the Victim position and found a Rescuer to join you in a dramatic exchange, you could be the one to switch first, say, into Persecutor and levy a harsh criticism of the Rescuer. That would invite the Rescuer to move into the newly vacant Victim position.

Or for example, if you were in the Victim position, being criticized by a Persecutor, after a few lashes you might switch to Persecutor yourself and wallop the person, thereby inviting him or her to take the now vacant Victim position.

Another example is when a Victim is being *discounted* by a Persecutor and a Rescuer rides into the scene ready to save the Victim.

Rescuers frequently wallop Persecutors, often to the dismay of Victims (an over-the-top reaction after all); so the Victim switches to Persecutor and the two join in a united initiative to pound out the Rescuer, who then moves to Victim. This was a common situation in domestic disputes when a single police officer arrived on the scene.

Another common switch is when a Rescuer gets fed-up with a Victim (tired of attempted rescues) and switches to Persecutor. You've perhaps heard the slogan 'don't blame the victim', and now you know how that happens. Blaming the victim (notice the lower case) is far less frequent compared to blaming the Victim (notice the upper case).

Most people on the drama triangle don't know they are, or that a switch is coming. So when it happens, it's a surprise.

And of course for an unaware Audience, the switch is also quite a dramatic turn of events. All participants have a moment of confusion -- "what the heck just happened?" This is quite appealing to an audience for reasons we'll get into next chapter; but have you noticed how the best dramatic theatrical and movie presentations are those with surprise twists and turns?

21

The switch also signals the final moments of transaction exchange that terminates the drama. After the switch, people will leave the drama triangle, or start a new one.

Feelings

Each of us has decided what our personal 'bad' and 'good' feelings are. Actually there are no 'good' or 'bad' feelings, just feelings we prefer not to experience or feelings we do prefer to experience.

For most people, sadness is a feeling we prefer not to have very frequently. Some people don't like feeling angry, and others dislike feeling anxious or afraid. Some of us don't like any of those. Many people like feeling happy and/or excited but in some family cultures feeling happy or excited is bad as in, "don't get your hopes up", or "don't enjoy this too much or something bad will happen", or "nothing good ever lasts."

As the transactions between drama roles proceed and the sequence approaches the switch, we can also anticipate the subsequent termination of transactions with all people experiencing a feeling reaction; usually but not always, feelings they'd rather not experience – the self-defined bad or negative ones. Some people finish a drama with what they define as a 'good feeling'.

We call *these predictable, repeated, familiar* feelings Racket Feelings, and they are part of the final pay-off of a drama.

Turning Up The Heat

A drama can be enacted at three levels of intensity. Like burns we describe the levels in 'degrees'; so we have 1st degree, 2nd degree, and worst of all, 3rd degree dramas [6].

1st degree dramas can be displayed in public or private, and the participants don't mind if there's an audience because the drama doesn't have severe, if any, social consequences.

2nd degree dramas tend to be enacted in private, and there would be, or are, significant social consequences if made public.

3rd degree dramas are enacted with severe consequences, usually life altering such as tissue damage. We say they're played for keeps, and at this level people often suffer physical harm.

Because there are people in the world who are victims and not in a drama in the Victim position, it's important to understand the difference – especially at this 3rd degree level.

Real victims do not discount themselves or play the 'poor me' song whereas Victims in drama will.

As such, an injured victim may not be a 3rd degree Victim. I mention this repeatedly because a Victim often steers their life to become a victim, and helping such a person from a Rescuer position perpetuates the drama. To be complete with this idea, a Victim can become a victim with any degree of intensity.

Dissecting the Samples

In chapter one I presented some examples of drama. Let's go back through them one by one and look for the discounts, the roles, the switch, and the racket feelings. To do this I'll type my comments indented and in italics below each transaction.

Sample 1: You're visiting with your friend Flora at the local coffee shop.

> *This example of drama we call, 'Yes But'. That's from Flora's point of view. It's called, 'I Was Only Trying To Help' from the listener or your point of view.*

Flora: "I just don't know what to do about Paul. He's so distracted by work these days that he never spends any time with us. I'm beginning to think he's a workaholic." *<Deep sigh>* "I'm really worried."

> *The opening sentence is a declaration of not knowing what to do about a situation, so it's not an overt self-discount; but the sigh is a give-away that Flora has taken the Victim position of 'poor me' with some kind of internal self-discount. By not making a request nor a clear statement of purpose for what she wants from the disclosure she is inviting you to get into drama.*

23

You: "Have you tried talking to him?"

> *Here's the first discount from you, the listener. Flora didn't ask for ideas, advice, or counseling; but you give it. Your psychological message is a discount of her something like, 'I agree, you are ineffectual. I on the other hand am full of good and helpful ideas; the most basic of which is, Have you tried talking to him?' With this transaction you've jumped into the Rescuer role.*

Flora: "Yes, of course, but he won't commit to a time when we can discuss it. He says it's all in my imagination."

> *Flora responds to your discount by declaring it to be of no help. This is her first 'Yes but.' She makes no requests nor states what she wants and thus remains a poor helpless me Victim with the implicit invitation to you to continue your efforts at a Rescue.*

You: "Have you tried counseling?"

> *So you try another helpful suggestion as a Rescuer who knows more than she does; discounting her problem solving capability again.*

Flora: "Yea, but the counselor said Paul had to come in as well."

> *And she does another 'Yes but.' Again, she makes no requests nor states what she wants and thus remains a Victim with the implicit invitation to you to continue your efforts at a Rescue.*

You: "Hmm, Hey, I know. Wayne Dyer has a great book" <interrupted>

> *Here's another piece of advice, batted away even before you finish giving it.*

Flora: "I can't read self-help books; Paul hates them and throws them out."

> *So you continue with another discount disguised as a Rescue effort.*

You: "Yea that's a problem. Well, you can always try the sexy approach?"

24

And Flora gives you a 'Yes but' once more.

Flora: <*weeping*> "I did, but he hardly noticed. I feel worse now. I don't want to talk about this anymore, as if you're the expert anyways."

> *Look at this one carefully. Flora begins this transaction as Victim but <u>switches</u> at the end into Persecutor with a mild discount of you.*

You: <*quietly*> "Sorry. I was only trying to help."

> *And you slide down the drama triangle into the now vacant Victim position and terminate the set of transactions with the slogan of the drama from your point of view, 'I was only trying to help'.*

Concluding this set of transactions, you and Flora both feel sad; which might be labeled as 'bad feelings'. Indeed, the mutual experience of 'bad feelings' at the end of a drama identify it as a drama. Sometimes a drama ends in 'good feelings' and in chapter three you'll discover why that is, but for now I'll say this: drama is a way of relating to others in a way that seems close, or intimate. Warning: even though drama has a strong taste, it's empty of nutrition.

Sample 2: You and your buddy Paul are sipping beers and watching the game Saturday afternoon. It's halftime and you casually start a conversation about your motor bike.

> *Similar to the previous example but a male version, from Paul's point of view we could call this, 'I Was Just Tryin to Help'. From your point of view we could call it. 'Na, tried that, didn't work. What else ya got?' The major difference from the last example is how the sequence starts in a subtle manner.*

You: "Yea, I was out on the bike last night."

> *A straight forward self-disclosure.*

Paul: "Beauty of a night for it."

> *A clear statement of opinion.*

You: "Woulda bin, I didn't get far."

Another self-disclosure but with an implicit invitation to inquire for details. This 'teaser' is the start of the drama from a Victim position with a psychological message something like, 'I got a story to tell but I'm not important/powerful enough to just say it clearly so you have to ask me to tell you.' It's a form of fishing.

Paul: "How come?"

And Paul bites.

You: "Runnin' rough."

Now that Paul's hooked, you can play with him; keep him tugging on your fishing line so you disclose your problem he can 'try' to solve.

Paul: "Dirty gas?"

So he plays along, struggling to get free, and makes his first foray into solving your motorbike problem as a Rescuer with the idea of dirty gas.

You: "Na, new gas filter, fresh gas."

But solving your problem isn't really what's going on. What's really happening is inviting him to discount you with his better-than-yours problem solving ideas. So you discount his latest idea. The implicit invitation to Rescue continues.

Paul: "Fouled plugs?"

Undeterred by a rejection, and fully invested in proving he can solve your problem, he ventures yet again into Rescuer mode.

You: "Na, swapped em out a week ago."

You bat his idea back.

Paul: "Air filter?"

He tries another rescue.

You: "Changed with the gas filter."

You brush that off like a mosquito on your nose.

Paul: "Well you probably need new rings, I keep tellin' ya man, get rid o' that rice burnin' crotch-rocket and get yourself a real ride!"

> *He delivers his biggest Rescue attempt, pulls out the big discount about your motorbike not being a 'real' motorcycle.*

You: "As if you're the expert. Meat head."

> *You've had enough playing with this fish so you pull a switcheroo into the Persecutor position and give him a poke.*

Paul: "Woa, easy now, I was just tryin' to help."

> *And he switches too, into Victim and declares the name of the drama from his point of view.*

Concluding this sequence, you're feeling angry and Paul is feeling hurt (which is either angry or sad or both). These are the 'bad feelings' for this drama.

Sample 3: Flora is already home when Paul comes into the kitchen.

> *In this sample, the drama from Flora's point of view is called, 'Kick Me.' And from Paul's point of view the drama is called, 'See What You Made Me Do.'*

Paul: *<Flops down on the sofa with a groan>*

> *The groan is either a physiological or psychological expression of discomfort and not necessarily anything more. But, like the sigh in sample 1 above, it could be an invitation for an inquiry from Flora, and if so is the first discount of himself by not asking directly for what he wants – such as attention.*

Flora: "Careful with that sofa. *<pause>* What's wrong with you?"

> *Flora either responds to the invitation or just starts the transaction exchange with an inquiry about Paul as a Victim.*

Paul: "Nothin."

> *Paul declines to self-disclose. If something is going on with him, this is a discount of himself.*

Flora: "Yea, right, all slumped and goofy face."

Flora doesn't believe him and expresses her evaluation of Paul as a Victim using the attribution that he is goofy faced. This is the first very clear discount as in, 'I know you better than you know yourself, and I say you have a goofy face, which means something is going on with you, and I wanna know what it is.' Because she is attempting to invite Paul into the Victim position (and perhaps he is already there on his own), we know she will be either in Rescuer or Persecutor, both of which discount the Victim.

Paul: "Messed up afternoon is all."

He discloses a bit of info; but not enough for Flora, or us, to know what was messed up. This is his first very clear overt discount of himself and his needs, as in, 'my messed up afternoon is not important enough to talk about'. So now we definitely know that his transactions leading up to this were also self-discounts and Paul is in the Victim position.

Flora: "I thought you and what's his name, Mr. Midlife Crisis were watchin' ball or playing with your bikes?"

Flora overtly discounts Paul's friend and then the activity they were engaged in. She has identified her position as Persecutor.

Paul: "It's tuning our bikes, not playing with our bikes. He got all pissy at me for no reason. So I split. Missed the end of the game. Left my damn beer over there."

Paul discounts himself again by claiming to not understand what happened.

Flora: "Well go back there and get it. We spent good money on that beer. It was the premium stuff too."

Flora tells him what to do, which is a clear discount of his problem solving capabilities. She also informs him the beer was valuable, which is a discount of his ability to evaluate purchases. These transactions are like jabs or pokes to Paul.

Paul: "I'm not crawling back there."

Paul discounts himself yet again by saying he would have to crawl if he did go to get his beer. Crawling is what infants do, so he's equating himself to an infant – reinforcing his Victimhood.

Flora: "Well you're not getting any more this week; we got a tight budget ya know, till someone around here gets some overtime."

And Flora jumps on that image to discount him further with a Parental threat, as if he's a child and mommy can deny him his fun food. She further discounts him with the word 'someone', as if he is just a non-identifiable person who earns income. This is another poke at him.

Paul: "Nag nag nag."

He's saying his interpretation of her transaction is that of nagging – he's discounting his ability to have boundaries from nagging. In other words, he's admitting to being poked.

Flora: "I wouldn't have to nag if you were any kind of real man."

Here's a full on discount of his manhood. A kick to the balls so to speak. Ouch.

Paul: <jumps up, strides right into her space> "Don't push me Flora."

The switch. He moves from Victim to Persecutor and discounts his ability to problem solve other than through intimidation (threat of violence).

Flora: "Or you'll what, go home to mommy?"

She's not quite done with the discounting of him yet and unwilling to switch positions with him. They both stand in the Persecutor position. It's just a temporary state. Someone will move off.

Paul: "Arggg" <punches the sofa>

Discounting himself and his problem solving capabilities, he resorts to violence. This is an escalation of the type of discounts that have been transacted so far – from verbal to physical. We discussed 'degrees' in detail in a previous section Turning Up The Heat. His punch is symbolic of what he'd like to do to Flora.

Flora: "Sorry, sorry."

> *Flora makes the switch of positions to Victim.*

Paul: "See what you made me do!" <storms out of the house>

> *Another discount, as if he has no control of himself – what a crock! And he moves back to Victim, another switch. Paul names his drama with this statement. By storming out of the house he's further discounting himself and Flora of being capable of problem solving.*

Flora: "Paul don't go, please honey I'm sorry I made you mad."

> *She makes the switch to Rescuer in accordance with his move to Victim. She pleads for him to stay. As Rescuer she discounts him by saying she 'made' him angry and therefore he's not responsible for himself.*

Concluding this drama, Paul is feeling angry and Flora is feeling sad. Like the other samples, these 'bad feelings' help us identify the sequence as a drama.

Sample 4: While Flora finishes preparing dinner, stepfather Paul is setting the table. Teenage daughter Celina wanders in with iPod jacked headphones blaring a head banger. She leans against the counter facing step-dad.

> *The name we use for this drama from Celina's point of view is, 'Let's You and Him Fight'. The first discount is from Celina with the loud music in a mutually shared physical space. This discount is her invitation to Flora and Paul to put her in the Persecutor position on the drama triangle. 'Let's get this drama started', so to say.*

Flora: "Paul will you ask her to shut that noise off. It's giving me a headache."

> *Flora opens the verbal sequence with two discounts. She first discounts her own ability to make a request of Celina. This is the setup for everything that follows; it's the bait. Another discount is her claim that the sound is creating a headache. If that was true both Paul and Celina would also be having headaches. No, the sound isn't responsible for Flora's*

headache. Both these discounts put Flora on the Victim position.

Paul: *<makes hand gesture indicating he wants daughter to cut the sound>* "Turn it off please."

Paul supports the discounts by complying with Flora's request; which means he has assumed the Rescuer role and agreed she is a Victim - since Celina is responsible for the noise, she is therefore also responsible for Flora's headache, and thus the implied discount of Flora. Celina is now truly established as the Persecutor.

As Rescuer, Paul makes his first foray into battle with the Persecutor on behalf of the damsel in distress.

Celina: *<makes a face, raising her voice>* "What?"

The Persecutor has an opportunity to discount the Rescuer with a 'face' and raising her voice, rather than problem solve, such as turning the sound off.

Paul: *<turning his voice volume up>* "Turn it off!"

Receiving these discount transactions, Paul escalates the transactional intensity of his rescue attempt by raising his own voice.

Celina: *<makes more of a face and upping her voice into a whine>* "What?"

Celina's most recent discount succeeded in engaging Paul more fully, so she uses the tactic again.

Flora: *<loudly>* "Oh for cryin' out loud, Paul don't just stand there, do something. She knows I get headaches from that crap."

Flora wades into the fray and admonishes Paul to be a better Rescuer. Her victimization includes a discount of Celina with the phrase, 'she knows I get headaches from that crap.'

Paul: *<reaches for the headphones, Celina does too, they have a brief struggle. Celina twists away and in so doing the headphone jack pulls from the iPod snapping the wire>*

The drama escalates up to another level that includes physicality.

Celina: *<headset off>* "Mom. Did you see that?"

Celina jumps into the Victim position. This is the switch. She appeals to Flora to move into the Rescuer role against the hopefully-soon-to-be Persecutor Paul.

Flora: "What? I saw you trying to give me a headache."

As with all dramas, when the switch happens, there is a moment of confusion for the players who didn't switch. Flora expresses this, and attempts to restore predictability by discounting Celina as before.

Celina: "He broke my iPod."

Celina is having none of that, she wants the Victim role. So she escalates by explicitly claiming Paul discounted her.

Flora: "What are you talking about?"

Flora is still reacting to the switch with confusion.

Celina: "Look, it's totally messed up."

So Celina cries poor me again.

Flora: "What?" *<turning to Paul>* "Did you?"

Now Flora makes her switch to Rescuer and questions Paul about the claimed discounts.

Paul: "That's ridiculous. It was an accident."

Paul has his moment of confusion about the switch of roles; but with both of the others switched over he is almost compelled to take the only open spot – the Persecutor. He declares his innocence, in a vain attempt to get the Victim role.

Celina: "Yea, right, an accident that happened exactly when you were grabbing for it."

But Celina has her position locked up.

Paul: "Well maybe if you didn't play that crap so loud that your mother gets a headache, we wouldn't have tried to get you to turn it down."

So Paul attempts to wiggle out of the Persecutor role by claiming Celina is the Persecutor.

Flora: "Paul, what's this <u>we</u> business? I didn't tell you to grab her iPod."

The Rescuer gets into the action with some interrogation of the Persecutor

Paul: "You're the one getting the headache."

And Paul the Persecutor is squirming; attempting to switch into Victim.

Celina: "You owe me an iPod." <storms out>

Celina senses a crowded role so leaves the drama with a great line, 'you owe me an iPod', thrown over her shoulder. She walks off the stage.

Paul: "Oh screw this noise. I was only trying to help you Flora. I'm goin' for a ride."

So Paul the Victim, walks off stage with a parting line as well.

Flora: "Feeling guilty? Pick up our beer from Mr. Midlife Crisis while you're out!"

And Flora moves fully into Persecutor throwing her own parting line as the curtain descends on this episode of the drama triangle.

Concluding this drama triangle are the 'bad feelings' experienced by Flora and Paul as anger. As for Celina, she exits the drama with a display of righteous indignation; which is anger as well; but blended with a moral and ethical message of superiority.

Sample 5: After taking her shower, Celina secludes herself in her bedroom. She's reviewing a 'look' her math teacher Ms. Davis gave her during class that afternoon. Using her diary, Celina writes the following:

> *What I invite you to notice about this sample is the drama Celina generates within the solo experience. The complete event is taking place in a mental and emotional space. No other real people are necessary for her to have a drama. Actually, that applies to all of us – we don't need others to run a drama triangle and get the payoff of our Racket Feelings. Playing solo can still be very dramatic.*

Princess Log, Stardate 5/4/2010 : 19:45 gmt

> *A discount is always accompanied by what we call grandiosity; which is an inflation of some aspect of self, others, or a situation. The two go hand in hand: discounts – grandiosity. So here we see an overt display of the grandiosity Celina is thinking: she's a princess.*

AlgaeBra gave me the dirty look again today. The gleaming...

> *The first discount is towards the math teacher who she nicknames AlgaeBra. A short time slot as Persecutor, Celina then goes on to discount herself by stating that a particular glance from the teacher was a 'dirty look'.*

...daggers of hatred flashed across the room, and I just barely had time to raise my shields and deflect the energy...

> *Celina has the capability to invent and put meaning on any event; yet she denies this power by attributing a quality, in this case dirty, to the glance. Further to this she builds a mental/emotional space that has 'daggers of hatred'. This is nonsense; but builds the inner drama and firmly puts Celina in Victim.*

...towards NerdBoy, who as usual was drawing photon torpedo circuit boards.

> *Next, comes the discount of a classmate with the nickname NerdBoy. This is a quick jump into Persecutor; but followed by a return to Victim in the statement 'She hates me ...'*

She hates me, I know it. I can feel it. What have I ever done to her? She marks me harder than the other girls. She never answers my questions. She frowns every time she looks my way. She's so mean. I'm so innocent.

34

Then follows a description of her Victimhood concluding with, 'I'm so innocent.'

That's it! She's jealous. I'm young, she's old. I'm beautiful, she's plain. I have a boyfriend, she's a divorcee. I have a whole wonderful life ahead of me, her life is half gone. Did I mention boobs, I have them and she doesn't. Maybe she's still single because men discover she's a Klingon? Nerdboy might know.

Now comes the switch of positions from Victim to Rescuer: 'That's it! She's jealous.' Rescuers can sound like Persecutors, except their cause is righteous, moral, ethical - saving a Victim from a Persecutor by beating up on the Persecutor.

This solo drama triangle terminates in typical 'bad feeling'. Celina exits with the familiar feeling we saw from her in the last example - righteous indignation (her racket feeling); a subtle anger of superiority; which brings us back to the idea that discounting always is accompanied by grandiosity. When I talk about scripts in the following chapter, remember back to how Celina concluded each of these dramas the same way.

Sample 6: After a quiet and tense dinner together, Celina gets up from the table and starts to leave the kitchen.

This is the version of drama triangle called 'Wooden Leg'; where a participant uses a disability or infirmity, perceived or real, to get on the triangle as a Victim.

Flora: "Where are you going? Take your dishes to the sink. I'm not your slave you know!"

Notice first the question, which isn't really a question; Flora doesn't want to know where Celina is going. In fact the question has a psychological message something like, 'Stop and pay attention to what I'm about to say.' Flora follows that command with an overt command, 'Take your dishes to the sink' and a statement of her inner experience of being Celina's slave and resenting it. This is the first discount, the belief that she could be someone's slave. What this discount includes is the covert discount message that Celina makes Flora a slave. It's a discount of Celina, thereby putting Flora on the Persecutor position.

Celina: <puts on a pouty face and returns to the table, then takes her dishes to the sink. She turns to leave the room>

> *Celina gets on the Victim position with her 'pouty face', as in 'I'm being persecuted as a slave master.'*

Flora: "Not so fast young lady. Get your butt over here. It's your damn turn to do the dishes."

> *Here comes another command, and as such a discount of Celina as a person worthy of receiving requests. Instead, Flora treats her like the slave she herself doesn't want to be.*

Celina: "Are you serious?"

> *Celina discounts Flora with a non-question; as if Flora would issue trivial commands. The covert message is something like, 'You can't order me around.'*

Flora: "My name is Flora, not serious; but I mean it, you're washing tonight!"

> *And Flora gives a non-answer discount right back.*

Celina: "Ha ha very funny; aren't you forgetting I have an allergy to latex?"

> *Celina now plays her big self-discount – she has a wooden leg disability and is therefore a Victim.*

Flora: "What's that got to do with washing dishes?"

> *Flora dismisses the claim of a wooden leg.*

Celina: "Washing dishes – hot water – latex gloves – hives."

> *Celina states the Victim position explicitly.*

Flora: "Start the water."

> *Flora issues a directive.*

Celina: "How can you expect anyone with a latex allergy to just go ahead and expose themselves to it."

Celina reasserts her Victimhood and explicitly states that Flora is a Persecutor.

Flora: "Washing dishes – hot water – bare hands – clean dishes."

Flora matches her. They're batting back and forth.

Celina: "Hot water makes my hands wrinkle and age. You want me to have old woman's hands? So I have to choose between hives and old woman's hands. You're so mean. You have no sympathy for someone with an allergy."

Celina escalates her Victimhood with another wooden leg. Now she has two, proving herself as a Victim. And she goes on to elaborate on Flora's Persecution.

Flora: "Oh forget it. I'll do it myself, like everything around here! "

Here's the switch. Flora goes to Victim, 'poor me'.

Wooden Leg can be a challenge to identify because usually the individual claiming Victimhood <u>does</u> have a disability or infirmity or injury or illness; something that does indeed limit their capability to respond to life's challenges. When a victim self-discounts, they go into the role of Victim on the drama triangle. At that point they have two challenges, the injury or disability or whatever, **and** the role of Victim.

Sample 7: Later that evening, as Flora is quietly reading, Celina approaches.

It's your turn with this one. Read the sample through and determine who is in what position, and if there was a switch, where was it and who switched to what. Then start again at the top and examine each transaction for discounts. Jot them down as I did underneath each transaction. I present my analysis just below.

Celina: "Can I talk to you about something really important?"

Flora: <*Noticing that Celina seems unusually quiet and polite, perhaps even sad, she sets her book down.*> "Sure honey, what's going on?"

Celina: <*Sits down beside Flora on the sofa, and starts to weep.*>

Flora: <*Softly*>, "What is it? What's wrong?"

Celina: "I wonder if you really care about me."

Flora: <*Feeling a sick twist in her stomach,*> "Of course I care about you. Why would you think such a thing?"

Celina: "Well, <*starting to cry*> you were pretty mean after supper."

Flora: <*Feeling apprehensive*> "Are you talking about the dish washing?"

Celina: "Yes. If you want me to move out so you can be alone with Paul you should just tell me."

Flora: <*Surprised.*> "Where did you get that idea?"

Celina: <*fully crying*> "It's obvious from how you both treat me."

Flora: "I don't want you to move out. I love you. That's a silly idea."

Celina: <*getting up off the sofa and walking away*> "You just don't understand me."

Flora: "Wait. Stay. Give me a chance to understand."

Chapter Summary

A great deal of drama between people can be understood as **discounting**. Discounting is the minimization or complete ignoring of information pertinent to a set of transactions between people. Discounting is a de-valuation of characteristics, traits, attributes or potentials of oneself, another person or persons, or a situation.

When this discounting takes place the people involved will take on a dramatic role. The roles available are **Victim**, **Persecutor**, or

Rescuer as active participants. The role of **audience** is a passive role that is also available.

A visual representation of these roles is the drama triangle. Typical of a **drama triangle** is the moment when participants switch roles. The switch is abrupt and often a surprise to those involved. One person switches first, say from Victim to Persecutor, and other participants feel a very compelling attraction to make a corresponding switch, say from Rescuer to Victim. Audience members usually remain in the role of Audience; although sometimes they get on the triangle in an active role.

Mission Possible

Using the chart you created in chapter one, go through the transactions one-by-one and identify the discounts, writing them in the right hand column. Identifying discounts is essential to the reduction of drama in your life. Once you've done that, identify the roles; and watch for the switch.

If you choose to continue with your real life example in missions to follow, you will increase the probability of reducing drama in your life beyond what reading alone will achieve.

Now you know how drama works. Next up, why we do it.

Ah, but first, my analysis of sample 7 above...

Sample 7: Later that evening, as Flora is quietly reading, Celina approaches.

Celina: "Can I talk to you about something really important?"

Celina starts the set of transactions with a clear request.

Flora: <*Noticing that Celina seems unusually quiet and polite, perhaps even sad, she sets her book down.*> "Sure honey, what's going on?"

Flora notices body language and assumes something is going on with Celina. Flora may be discounting by thinking something is wrong with Celina.

Celina: <*Sits down beside Flora on the sofa, and starts to weep.*>

Celina could be simply sharing how she's feeling, or this could be a Victim inviting a Rescue.

Flora: <*Softly*>, "What is it? What's wrong?"

Flora rescues. The discount is that Flora doesn't wait for Celina to make a request. Instead she send is a message such as, 'There there poor dear, since you are incapable of activating yourself, I'll do it for you.' Notice that Flora does this, softly, since tender little helpless Victims are so vulnerable.

Celina: "I wonder if you really care about me."

Sounds like a question; but it isn't! In fact it's a statement about her mental activity. It's a self-disclosure about her wondering. By phrasing it the way she did, Celina may be inviting Flora to once again discount her ability to ask a question directly.

Flora: <*Feeling a sick twist in her stomach,*> "Of course I care about you. Why would you think such a thing?"

Flora jumps in and Rescues by answering an unasked question. The sick twist in her stomach could be her intuition informing her that in this drama, she has just been identified as the Persecutor.

Celina: "Well, <*starting to cry*> you were pretty mean after supper."

Celina overtly declares her Victimhood by Flora, the Persecutor.

Flora: <*Feeling apprehensive*> "Are you talking about the dish washing?"

Flora is feeling the fear of an accused, a Persecutor, about to be sentenced, without having any defense.

Celina: "Yes. If you want me to move out so you can be alone with Paul you should just tell me."

Celina reveals her Victimhood idea that Flora truly is a Persecutor. Not only does Flora want to be alone with Paul but she is dishonest by not telling Celina to her face. The fantasy discount that Celina is telling herself to feed this idea is probably something about not being loveable.

Flora: <*Surprised.*> "Where did you get that idea?"

> *Flora doesn't want to be in Persecutor and attempts to get out of it with a request for evidence.*

Celina: <*fully crying*> "It's obvious from how you both treat me."

> *Celina's having none of that, discounting herself internally with secret evidence that keeps her in Victim state.*

Flora: "I don't want you to move out. I love you. That's a silly idea."

> *Flora attempts yet again to get out of Persecutor; but not very skillfully because she discounts Celina's idea as silly.*

Celina: <*getting up off the sofa and walking away*> "You just don't understand me."

> *Here's the switch. Celina goes from Victim to Persecutor with her discount of Flora. Is it possible Celina is once more expressing some righteous indignation, her racket feeling?*

Flora: "Wait. Stay. Give me a chance to understand."

> *So Flora too switches, from Persecutor to Victim.*

Chapter 3

Dramatic Purpose

The Reasons For Drama

There are five reasons people get involved in drama,

1. to exchange what are called strokes
2. to attain the illusion of emotional intimacy
3. to reinforce and/or follow certain beliefs about themselves, others or their reality
4. to confirm or reinforce a fundamental belief called the life position
5. and how to structure time

Each person in a drama will have a hierarchy of these reasons for any particular sequence.

For example, Flora's main reason for drama in sample one is most likely stroke exchange, but in sample three she says, "I wouldn't have to nag if you were any kind of real man." This reveals a belief about men that she has just seemingly proven to be true.

Some people don't care why they think, feel, or do a particular thought, feeling, or behavior. If that's your stance, skip on to chapter four where we get into the strategy and tactics of refusing invitations for drama and/or getting off the stage if and when we find ourselves in a drama.

Personally I like knowing the underlying reasons for why because it helps me change myself. If you're curious about the why we do drama, in no specific order, here are some details.

To Exchange Strokes

Suppose you turn to a wall and say, "Hey you!" Normally, a wall won't reply, so you don't know if you actually exist, that is, you didn't influence the wall to acknowledge you as separate from it. If you turn to a human being and say, "Hey you," the probability is the person will respond back to you. Now you know that you are in some form of existence because you influenced a response from the environment.

When one of us recognizes the existence of another, it's called a 'stroke'.

Verbal strokes - "Good Morning," "Hello," "uh hu," "hey you," "get lost," "screw off," and hundreds more.

Body language strokes - eye contact, smiles, frowns, nods, touch, eye brow raising, shrugs, and dozens more.

Knowing you exist is psychologically very important; so important that you'll engage in drama to get a response from the environment. Getting strokes is one of the primary reasons people get into drama.

The theory is that recognition of existence is a basic human psychological need.

Research in child development suggests that strokes are necessary to infants for actual physical survival. Even if a stroke isn't a basic human need most people would agree that recognition of existence is important.

Strokes are experienced on a scale from most pleasurable to most painful.

For example, receiving sexual pleasure from your lover is a set of strokes at one end of the spectrum, and receiving a beating from a bully is a set of strokes at the other end.

Both are strokes and what we know is that people will seek **any** form of stroke even if painful rather than go without. And the stroke can be either physical or verbal. Verbal strokes are symbolic of a physical one, so verbal strokes are not quite as satisfying as physical strokes.

We call the pleasurable strokes *positive,* and the painful strokes *negative.*

Our parents preferred to give us certain kinds of strokes as we grew up. They also delivered strokes in specific quantities. If the supply was stable, these kinds and quantities of strokes are what we became comfortable and accustomed to. As adults now, we continue to prefer and seek out these forms and quantities, even if they are negative or in short supply. Therefore, a man or woman typically marries someone who delivers a stroke profile similar to what they received from their parents. In the case of negative stroke patterns, as observers we often wonder how someone puts up with such abuse, is aware of it, lamenting it, perhaps even hating it, yet remaining in the relationship. In some cases, people reframe the abuse as a sign of caring. And indeed from a stroke perspective the abuser cares about the abused enough to pay attention and deliver negative strokes.

This brings us back to the fact that negative strokes are better than no strokes.

A child proves self-existence because the parents respond: the child exists to the parents. He or she must exist and matter enough to the parents because the parents are responding with strokes. A child receiving no strokes, no recognition at all, feels emotionally abandoned at best and nonexistent at worst, usually with significant psychological implications. With infants it is known as anaclitic depression, and hospitalism when fatal.

Up to this point I've only talked about person to person strokes, or what we call *interpersonal strokes.*

If interpersonal strokes are in short supply we will seek out intrapsychic/virtual (fantasy) strokes. These are called intrapsychic because they take place inside oneself; the inner part of us recognizes the existence of the outer part. This may include actual touching. Much of the appeal of daydreaming is in the delivery of intrapsychic strokes. Pornography is appealing for its assistance in creating a daydreaming space for the delivery of intrapsychic strokes. Masturbation is a way of making intrapsychic strokes physical.

In the movie Cast Away, Tom Hank's character is marooned and isolated on a South Seas island without any method of receiving strokes. He needs strokes, so he invents an imaginary playmate -

Wilson The Volleyball, with whom he exchanges strokes. The strokes are of course intrapsychic, projected onto Wilson. The strokes' psychological value isn't sufficient to sustain the guy; which eventually motivates him to leave the island.

Looking in the mirror before going to a social function is a sequence of intrapsychic stroking, perhaps negative: "You look fat," perhaps positive "You handsome fellow," and if another person is willing to engage in interpersonal verbal stroking, so much the better.

A large number of people have pets in order to secure a source of strokes for themselves. These aren't as good as human strokes but they fill the bill somewhere between interpersonal and intrapsychic. If an animal has the mental capabilities to deliver what we perceive as human type strokes, the animal is often a more favorable pet.

For many people, dogs are preferred over snakes or frogs as pets because the former acknowledge us with overt behavior we evaluate as recognition. For example we walk in the room and Fido wags her tail as a canine hello – close enough to an interpersonal stroke. Snakes and frogs are probably just as aware of our presence as dogs, and acknowledge us in 'snakey' or 'frogy' ways; but not in ways we humans perceive and evaluate as recognition, so we don't receive strokes from them as we do with dogs. With either type of pet we could decide to fantasize some strokes as in, "Ah the snake is smiling at me," these would be intrapsychic.

For optimum health, each of us need both positive and negative strokes. I know this might sound a bit weird at first but follow along because it's important.

You and I, as does every child, know deep down that we are not totally acceptable to all people. If we only experience positive strokes we know that we do not have a realistic picture of ourselves as others see us. Therefore we must hear some negative strokes to validate the authenticity of our experience of reality. Negative strokes also validate and give relative meaning to the positive strokes we receive. Furthermore, we need to receive negative strokes to gain an appreciation for thoughts, feelings and behaviors that are unhealthy, dysfunctional, or anti-social.

Can you start to appreciate the importance of drama stroke exchanges?

Since we all need them, want them and exchange them, a kind of economy has developed using strokes as currency[7]. As with all economies, the **stroke economy** has some rules. The basis of the following rules is that strokes are in short supply. This is a handy mistaken belief (not actually a fact) for behavior management purposes especially for the control of children. If strokes are scarce, they can be given out like prizes for good behavior, or like slaps for bad behavior.

Here are the five dysfunctional stroke economy rules. If you decide to break these rules, be prepared to feel better both mentally and physically. Be ready to get along better with others, deepen your relationships with people, always have something to say in social situations, and probably feel more self-confident in any social situation. Plus, you'll develop immunity to drama.

Rule #1: **Do Not Give Strokes Openly or Freely**: The mistaken belief underlying this rule is that strokes, especially positive strokes, are rare and must be hoarded like cookies. So of course if we believe that, we won't give strokes freely and willingly – and then they actually do become scarce. Once scarce, they are given only for special occasions, for special purposes, or with special intentions. With negative strokes, we use various methods of delivery or hiding their delivery such as 'constructive criticism' or back handed complements.

Rule #2: **Do Not Accept A Stroke Given To You because (oh oh) accepting it might mean or imply an agreement to some ulterior contract:** The meaning we assign to accepting a stroke is, more often than not, a guess or a fantasy as to the intention of the person giving the stroke.

A common example is when a sales person gives you a complement. Is it genuine or part of the sales pitch?

Similarly in couples counseling I hear wives say they don't trust complements from their husbands because it's given only as a prelude for sex. A smile exchanged between two people can be interpreted in a thousand ways all of which are fictional until confirmed by reality testing; but most people accept their fictional interpretation as fact and live in that reality.

Discounting a stroke – "really, you like this dress on me?", or outright refusing to accept it – "what are you talking about, this dress is ugly" require little effort compared to reality testing – "what do you like about my dress?"

Another method of removing the value of a stroke is to pass it on to others – "oh you look lovely too." The presentation of the Oscar film awards is a simple demonstration of this rule. Each stroke/award is followed by a series of 'thank you' strokes that psychologically balance the recipient's stroke economy. Anyone who dares break this rule is judged rude, or worse – selfish. Can you imagine an Oscar recipient simply walking on stage, accepting the statuette, turning to the audience and saying, "Thank you for this award. It means a lot to me," and then walking off stage?

***Rule #3:* Do Not Ask For Strokes - Even If You Want Them**: Here's a wild mistaken belief: if you have to ask for a stroke, it's a sure sign of some character flaw or personality defect, such as weakness.

Here's another mistaken belief: asking for strokes proves that you're 'needy', and a needy person is a flawed or bad person. And yet another mistaken belief: the person you ask for the stroke will not be authentic if they give you a stroke - they're just doing it to be polite, so really, the stroke is of no value. Some people also mistakenly think asking for strokes is demeaning and they won't 'stoop' to that - just like not asking for directions when you're lost.

Asking for strokes is a taboo thing to do. People who ask for strokes may be considered rude, needy, or clingy at worst and perhaps simply weird at best. And many people mistakenly believe that if they have to ask for strokes, doing so renders worthless whatever strokes they do receive. Naturally this false belief is accompanied by its sister belief that says, "If you really loved me or cared about me, you'd know what I need and I wouldn't have to ask." So when you put the two rules together, they form a tight injunction against asking for strokes.

When we were infants and young children, our parents did appear to magically 'mind read' our needs and deliver them to us, proving their love along the way. But as adults, the mind reading method has a very low probability of success. A conscious adult, being responsible for getting his or her needs met in appropriate and effective methods will ask for strokes from those people most likely to be willing to give them. Like asking for a cool glass of water on a hot summer day, the satisfaction comes from fulfilling a need, not from waiting for someone to notice you've passed out.

Rule #4: **Do Not Refuse A Negative Stroke:** If you get a stroke you don't want, do not refuse it.

There are several mistaken beliefs under this rule such as,

- You'd be rude to refuse a negative stroke;
- Negative strokes are for your own good;
- Saying no to a negative stroke will cause a fight;
- "I probably deserve it and don't even know it."

A question I hear frequently is, "what's the difference between constructive criticism and a negative stroke?"

In the following chapter I talk about contracting as a method of avoiding drama so I don't want to jump ahead too much; so the brief answer is they are the same except for context. If a person has requested thoughtful comments, including negative strokes, then the context is contractual and a drama is less probable.

Rule #5: **Do Not Give Yourself Any Strokes**: If you do, you could be accused of bragging which of course is believed to be rude! You might also be labeled egotistical or egocentric or even narcissistic - which is believed to be bad. And worst of all for many people, you'd be labeled selfish!

Do you recognize any mistaken beliefs in those examples?

For most people, their stroke economy is precariously maintained. Following the stroke rules just described keeps us in a perpetual state of stroke deprivation – so, we get into drama.

Remember the switch I talked about in the last chapter, well, the person who pulls it first has filled their stroke quota; and the stroke exchanges are no longer needed – for the time being.

For the Illusion of Emotional Intimacy

Intimacy is the capacity to relate to another person in an honest emotionally open equal and caring way that includes dialogue, transparency, vulnerability and reciprocity.

Intimate relationships create a social network that provides strong emotional attachments and fulfill our need for belonging and to be cared for.

For most of us, our first experience of closeness was with mother. We were physically close – actually attached for nine months. We were open to her, transparent it seemed, and had no secrets from her, we were vulnerable and she delivered all our needs (or else I wouldn't be writing this and you wouldn't be reading this.) We belonged and we were cared for. Soooo nice.

The two big pieces that are missing from this relationship are equality and reciprocity; which is why it wasn't true intimacy as defined above. But when closeness took place it was good – in a grandiose, narcissistic fashion.

How can we get back to that Garden of Eden of closeness?

Find a romantic partner who agrees to be mommy again; or (drum roll) get some drama happening. People involved in drama often feel open, exposed, vulnerable, and transparent. They self-disclose feelings and depths of themselves normally sequestered away. There's passion and juice, brutal honesty, telling it like it is, letting it all hang out. But there are some missing pieces of real intimacy. Equality, and reciprocity are removed by the discounting that takes place.

But it's close to intimacy; and close is good enough for many folks so they jump into drama.

To Reinforce Beliefs

Imagine for a minute that when you were a young child, you asked yourself the question, "What will my life be like?" And because, like all children, you had a zesty creative imagination, you proceeded to invent a story about how a person such as you actually lived a life. The invention was a kind of mini fairy story, adventure novel, tragic drama, happy musical or dark horror mystery. Being in a particular family and a surrounding culture, your story would be greatly influenced by the family story or the cultural story.

Throughout human history, thoughtful observers have theorized that we humans actually write this story over a period of formative years.

Therapists call this outline a narrative, or a **life script**. Our script includes an idea about how our story will shape up and how we'll ship out (die).

Untold hours of clinical observation by therapists tend to support the theory, and the theory has been a helpful foundation for personal growth, problem solving, and therapeutic change for millions of people around the world. Have you ever said or heard someone say, "Oh yea, it's the story of my life?"

Right from the get-go we make decisions (explanations) about our subjective experience of life. These get welded into our script as beliefs. Our set of beliefs makes up a huge section of what we experience as reality.

Some very common examples I've heard in my psychotherapy practice include...

> I am, or you are: (take your pick) stupid, sickly, ugly, clumsy, unlovable, flawed, cute, sweet, sexy, smart, a princess/prince, a nothing.

> To be loved I, or you, have to: (take your pick) be perfect, be strong, try hard, please you, hurry up.

> To get the goodies in life, I or you, need to: (take your pick) lie, cheat, take what I want, be sneaky, tell you a story, sell you a story, convince you, manipulate you, be smarter than you, outsmart you, be secretive, hide from you, struggle with you, seduce you.

> To succeed in life I or you need to be right, do the right thing, and correct 'wrongs'. This is called the **righting response** and is a very compelling belief.

> To get attention from the world I, or you, have to: (take your pick) be ill, be helpless, be hopeless, be incompetent, be naughty, be loud, be impudent, make noise, break rules, start conflicts, be nice, be compliant, be accommodating, give up what I want, say nice things, be polite no matter what, use words to settle conflict, always be truthful, always answer questions.

> Other people are (take your pick) enemies, liars, cheaters, untrustworthy, dangerous, out to get me, selfish, better than me, more worthy than me, more loveable than me, have all

the fun, get all the luck, have more (whatever) than me, are more deserving than me.

The world is (take your pick) full of evil, dangerous, out to get me, oblivious to me, inert, dead, just a dream, benign, nurturing, kind, loving, supportive, helpful to me.

Once we make a script decision, we tend not to examine it for validity thereafter. Instead, we document its existence every time we can – in other words, we prove again and yet again that it's a truth. We are highly resistant to acknowledging that it's a decision. People will fight tooth and nail to defend the 'truth' of their core script beliefs.

Getting into drama is a great way to set up a proving. This is what Flora was doing with her statement, "I wouldn't have to nag if you were any kind of real man." She'd made a decision about men long ago that is now a belief; held as a truth. The drama she and Paul engaged in proved her belief.

From the examples above, there is one belief I see in my work over and over that I think is especially worthy of bringing to your attention.

Called the righting response it's the belief that something incorrect must be corrected as in, "let me correct you on that". For example, misuse of vocabulary by one spouse is commonly knee-jerk-corrected by the other.

Here's a sample:

Greg: "I was fishing just west of second line this evening and a fly fisherman waded down the river to me. He was so osteotentaciously outfitted I almost laughed."

Barbara: "You mean ostentatiously."

> *Barbara obviously knew the word Greg was intending. She got the meaning; but she was compelled to fix the sentence with the correct word because she has a belief that incorrect vocabulary needs correcting. Perhaps she is also proving herself smarter or more articulatorious (chuckle).*

Another version of the righting response (to be correct) is to avoid being wrong. Many people experience shame from not being right, or being discovered as not right. Much drama between people, groups, even nations is founded on the desire to live by the belief that being right is the only way. Here's how that looks, continuing on from the sample above with both people wanting to avoid being incorrect:

Greg: "Yea that's what I said ostentatiously."

Barbara: "No, you said osteotentaciously, which isn't a word."

Greg: "I know it's not a word, which is why I said ostentatiously, not whatever it was you just said I said."

Barbara: "We didn't record it; but you did say osteotentaciously."

Greg: "Whatever."

To Confirm Our Life Position

One of the fundamental, perhaps the first, script decision we make is a primordial sense of self okness: either I am ok, or I'm not ok.

Likewise we make a decision about the world being ok or not ok. With these two decisions made, we have what's called our *existential position*. It's on this platform that a complete script edifice is constructed.

For example, if I decided that I was not ok (I-) then subsequent decisions would tend to be negatively biased about myself. From the chart of belief examples above I'd probably decide I was unlovable, stupid, sickly, flawed; that I needed to hide myself, that I had to be sneaky to get what I wanted, that I was naughty, and so on. I would probably engage in drama that confirmed those beliefs and thus reinforce the I- foundation.

Suppose I decided that the world was not ok (we call this "you're not ok," or U-) then subsequent decisions about others and the world would tend to be negatively biased. From the chart above, I'd probably decide other people were liars, cheats, selfish, untrustworthy and the world was dangerous, doomed, full of sinners, cold heartless and oblivious of me. I might use the phrase, "It's a dog eat dog world!" I would be baffled by those who think the universe is abundant and loving (the U+ position).

This existential position has four possible outcomes based on I'm ok (I+) or not ok (I-) and the world is ok (U+) or not ok (U-). One of the purposes of drama is to prove the position we decided on.

By proving the position, we make life more predictable and thus reinforce the illusion of our ability to have control over it.

Now that you know this, you might choose to listen for clues about what a person's life position might be. Even more importantly, listen to yourself and assess what your position is. Listen especially closely during drama for clues about yourself. The healthy position of I+U+ is a beautiful place to reside since it does not include discounts, or drama.

To Structure Time

How we interact with each other over time is called **Time Structuring**. There are six ways people spend time together. As you read the following list, keep in mind from above that one of the purposes of transacting with another is the exchange of strokes. So, each form of time structuring has an associated intensity of stroke. Withdrawal is at the low end, intimacy is at the high end. Drama fits just below intimacy. Therefore, one way to get out of drama, is to change the time structure.

1. *Withdrawal* is when a person either physically or emotionally (or both) leaves and in so doing refuses to engage in any transactions. As such the only strokes they can exchange are with themselves. The person may have decided that the risk of negative strokes outweighs the benefits of receiving positive strokes. So, internally, the person may experience a lot of self-talk, a day dream, or take a snooze. Regardless, his or her stroke economy will not benefit from the situation. It's like trading money with yourself.

2. *Rituals* in the context of time structuring are highly structured, prescribed or pre-programmed sequence of transactions designed to produce predictable stroke exchanges. There is a perceived higher risk of negative strokes than withdrawal; however the high probability of attaining the predicted positive strokes makes the risk acceptable. Rituals include the various greetings we engage in such as, "Hi. Hi", hand shaking, "How are you?", "How ya doin?", waving, and

smiling. These simple acts are important sources of strokes - like exchanging five dollar bills with each other.

3. **Pastimes** are sequences of transactions that are familiar and somewhat predictable to the participants but not as structured as rituals. Pastimes are always conversational with no action component, and often about times past. The light superficial conversation people engage in when meeting for the first time is usually *pastiming*. Talking about the weather, cars, sports, and the economy are typical male pastimes in western culture. Similarly, female pastimes include 'the children', diets, Oprah or pop stars. In terms of strokes, there is less predictability of a positive exchange; but either way, the exchange will be more intense than a ritual exchange; like exchanging ten dollar bills instead of fives. Another reason for pastiming is to check each other out for future engagement in even more intense time structures.

4. **Activities** are transactions directed at achieving a material goal. Talking may be involved but time is devoted to producing a result. An activity is 'active'. For example, playing a sport, fixing something, making a meal, a goal directed business meeting, or taking a hike are all activities. The activity is a here & now event. In terms of strokes, while some will be exchanged during the activity, usually an intense exchange is made at the close of the activity. Thus it is a time delayed exchange. The types of strokes that are exchanged is often dependent on a positive or negative assessment of goal achievement - like an exchange of five, ten or twenty dollar bills depending on the perceived group value of the goal; or even fines levied in various amounts for failure to perform.

5. **Drama** is the next level of stroke intensity and method of structuring time with others[8]. Drama always has ulterior transactions, meaning a psychological level message is attached to the social level message. As we saw in the previous chapter, the ulterior message is a discount. The exchange of negative strokes is often fast, deep, and painful. Sort of like getting hit with one or several $100 dollar fines, bang bang bang. One way to exit a drama is to change your time structure.

6. **Intimacy** is at the top of the stroke exchange time structure hierarchy. The transactions are simple, honest and authentic self-disclosures as opposed to the out-of-awareness

transactions with drama (where the players put responsibility for their feelings on others).

Intimacy is the capacity to relate to another person in an honest emotionally open, equal, and caring way that includes dialogue, transparency, vulnerability and reciprocity.

Intimate relationships create a social network that provides strong emotional attachments and fulfill our need for belonging and to be cared for.

In intimacy, each person takes responsibility for their own feelings.

Chapter Summary

Getting into drama is a way to get strokes, lots of them, reliably. It's a way to structure time, that is - something to do; and drama gives an approximation of intimacy. Drama proves our existential position and beliefs about ourselves and the world around us; which then allows us to live our script with false confidence that we know what life is all about – after all, it's written right there in the script. Drama is a method for living according to our beliefs.

Mission Possible

Pull out your personal drama chart you started in chapter one. You added the discounts, roles and switch discussed in chapter two. Your mission this time is to look for clues about the reasons you got on that triangle. Remember, there could be several reasons. Tip: stroke exchange is almost always involved. Take your best guess about your life position (I'm ok or not ok; others are ok or not ok). Look for beliefs you 'needed' to live by or prove.

Chapter 4

You've Had It Up To Here

Stepping Out of Drama & Refusing Invitations

The Ketchup Story: My wife and I were at Point Pelee National Park for our annual week of spring migration birding. One day, while I sat at a picnic table beside the hamburger stand, intent on eating lunch, a dapper elderly gentleman sat down beside me to drink a tea. An elderly woman, unknown to me or the gentleman, sat down as well, across from us.

I noticed she had binoculars suspended by a neck strap, resting on her belly. I saw too that her hands were disfigured in the manner common to arthritis. Indeed, she held her hotdog with the typical awkwardness of that affliction. Her first bite squirted ketchup over the napkin down the right sleeve of her jacket. The man beside me started the series of transactions which, to the best of my memory went something like this (keep in mind we're all strangers to each other):

Man: "Careful now, you dripped Ketchup."
Woman: "Can't be helped. It will wash."
Man: "Better cover your binoculars though."
Woman: "They'll wash too."
Man: "Just slip then under your jacket."
Woman: *<Sighs, then puts her hotdog on the table and begins an attempt to unzip her jacket. This requires significant effort with her deformed hands and fingers. Many sighs and mutterings ensue.>*
Man: *<Reaches over to assist.>*
Woman: "Don't!" *<Glares at him.>*
Man: *<Withdraws his hands.>* "Just trying to help."
Woman: *<Picks up her hotdog and takes a bite. Ketchup oozes into the napkin, clinging to it with seemingly miniscule Newtonian physics. She looks at that, pauses, then sets the hotdog back on the table and examines her binoculars.>*

Me:	"Do you need help?"
Woman:	"Yes."
Me:	"What can I do to help?"
Woman:	"Can you take my binoculars off?"
Me:	"Sure." *<I get up, walk around behind her, lift off the binoculars and set then on the table.>*
Woman:	"Thank you."
Me:	"You're welcome."

Notice how the Man discounted the Woman to start the drama. Notice how it proceeded very quickly to a switch from him as Rescuer and her being Victim, to him being a Victim of her persecutory glare. Notice how my interaction with her is completely different – no drama.

That's what you'll learn to do in this chapter – drama free interactions.

The last chapter described some very powerful and compelling reasons to get involved in drama. To drastically reduce any temptation for drama, I invite you to address those reasons. Good psychotherapy is an excellent method of doing that; but for our purpose here, as a do-it-yourself guide, I have good news and bad news.

The good news is that there is only one attitude change, and a trio of behaviors you need to change to drastically reduce drama. I won't state that you'll be drama free, but you will be a long way down that road. Furthermore, if or when you engage a therapist to empower yourself into the drama free zone, you'll be well prepared. The bad news is you have to practice and practice and practice to antidote the habits that currently get you involved in drama.

Here's the trio of behaviors:

1. Stop discounting.
2. Set clear contracts and boundaries.
3. Ask for what you want in a clearly understood way.

Getting out of drama means you use inner resources to conduct problem solving instead of using those resources for drama.

The more often you decline invitations for drama, the more time and energy you can invest in actually solving problems or challenges when you or someone else is a real victim.

Furthermore, you may have significant challenges to face as you age and approach death. If you've spent your whole life playing Victim and doing drama and thereby **not** honing your skills as a problem solver, you'll be quite unprepared for problem solving those ageing, dying, and death issues.

Stop Discounting:

The Essential Foundation of No More Drama

How many times in your life did you face a decision that stopped you in your tracks because you didn't know which way was best?

Nobody else knows you better than yourself – all the secret thoughts and desires, dreams and goals, 'good' thoughts about others, 'bad' thoughts about others, the lies and cheats, corners and close calls, the errors and mistakes swept hidden away, the real reasons for doing and not doing. Nobody else has a clue about that material.

And there's even a lot **you** don't know about yourself, right?

Like, why you can't lose weight, why you can't stand a messy kitchen, why you resist another person's ideas, why don't you have more friends? And so on.

So when you, *the expert about you*, are stopped in your tracks by a challenge and you don't know which way to go, how the heck can anyone else, a non-expert about you, saunter by your life and toss in a quick appropriate piece of "here, I know what you should do"? Think about that.

Flip it around: how can you saunter by someone else's life and throw out a quick piece of "I know what you should do"?

Discounting others stops when you make an attitude change; an admission that **you truly don't know what's ultimately best for another person**.

Read that bold bit again...

I'll say this slightly differently. Ground yourself with a mental attitude that you don't actually know what's optimal for another person.

Just because you're smarter or more educated or you know a lot more than that person over there doesn't mean you have God-like divination powers to know what's ultimately best. Even if you are the smartest person on the planet, you don't know everything about that person in order to make a decision about what's best. Having all information about another person is impossible for a human being.

Maybe this is why most health care providers require informed consent from the client/patient – because knowing all is impossible.

In the Ketchup Story above, the man assumed he knew what was best for the woman so he dove overboard for the Rescue. Wrong assumption, and she set him straight – the binoculars will wash off.

But for you die-hard Rescuers who really believe you should give advice and counsel to that person over there on the Victim position, I propose this:

> *Once you know yourself and the ethical, moral, psychological reasons why you think, feel, and do everything (such as wanting to give advice), then start in on knowing someone else to the same degree. And when that's achieved, then start on the project of knowing that person's social culture to the same degree in order to approach some ideas about optimal choices.*

Rescuers, I invite you to give up on the advice – it's discounting. Get on with your own life, that's a full time project by itself.

Many of you reading this are parents, so here are a few words for consideration.

If you continually discount your children, they'll learn how to be Victims; that is, they will learn how to sing the Blues and wait for a Rescuer to come along. They'll not learn how to figure out what they want and how to ask questions in order to deliver to themselves their wants. Females learn how to remain helpless waifs waiting for Prince Charming to come home from the world each evening and take care of them. Males learn how to remain mamma's boys, waiting for mommy to pack their lunch, kiss their cheek and send them off to work each day.

Do you know any grown males or females who live as if they're still children and need their spouse to be the parent?

Since I'm talking about parenting, a parent's role is to prepare a child for independence; meaning self-responsibility, and self-accountability. Parenting is a tapered role. It declines as a child gains knowledge and skills about how to figure out what they want, and how to ask questions about getting their wants. When a parent goes Rescuing (discounting a child), the child suffers.

Instead, encourage and acknowledge problem solving.

Consider that in matters of Victimhood, you must honor the Victim's ability, capability, potential, and probability to ask for what they want once they decide to problem solve.

They may not actually know what they want or what's best for themselves yet; so that's their task – to figure it out.

They may not know how to ask for what they want; in which case, learning how to ask is their task.

They may not know who to ask, so that's their task – finding out who to ask for what they want.

If the person truly wants to solve a problem, they will not be on the Victim position.

Let's go back to the Ketchup Story...

When the woman examined her napkin with the Ketchup ready to drip off and she didn't sigh, I thought she might be off the Victim position, and perhaps engaging in problem solving.

I asked her a clear question, "Do you need help?"

Her answer was clear as well, with no hint of Victim. I asked her for a specific directive, "What can I do to help?" No discount. No attempt to mind read her. She's the closest anyone can be to an expert on

61

herself. How would I, could I possibly know what's best for her. Maybe she needs to learn and practice how to ask for help from strangers while sitting in a non-Victim position.

If you help a chick peck its way out of its shell, it will die within minutes – it needs to peck itself out and that's a fact! Look it up. I saw this myself one time. Family members had just helped the last chick get free of its shell in order to not be left behind by the hen, who was leading the other ten chicks out the door into the barnyard. Chick took a dozen steps and toppled right over, dead! Chicks need to peck themselves out in order to stimulate organs and tissues into full functionality.

Shortcuts can be fatal.

Same with Victims - they need to peck themselves out. You cannot do it for them! Doing so is not a favor but a grave disservice and insult – a discount – wherein you are covertly saying to them, "I agree with your self-discount, yes you are a helpless waif and pathetic little human being; and I the great Rescuer know-it-all God wanna-be up here in my high-chair, shall solve your problem."

For those of you who live your life in the Rescuer role, these last paragraphs could be shocking. I invite you to take a breath. You can choose to retire yourself from that lifestyle.

FACT: A Victim isn't involved in drama to solve a problem. A Victim may be singing the Blues with such convincing melody that local mourning doves coo in harmony; but the problem they're singing about is just a façade covering the underlying reasons discussed in the last chapter.

For those of you who put yourself in the Victim position; meaning, you discount yourself I invite you to consider the following questions:

a) Have you ever decided what you want and don't want?

b) Have you ever asked a question?

If the answer is yes to both questions then you have the capability to figure out what you want in life situations and you know how to ask questions about how to get what you want.

Ponder this for a minute.

Because you can ask questions, you can seek out experts for answers. Going to experts for answers is vastly different from asking your best friend for advice. Unless your best friend is an expert on the subject matter.

If I ate a chocolate bar for every time I heard about marital advice being dispensed by people who aren't experts I'd be the size of a blue whale. Just because someone has experienced <whatever> does not make them a <whatever> expert!

So if you're serious about problem solving, seek an expert to answer your questions.

So, Victims, get on with figuring out what you want and how to get it.

And one more thing: forgiveness has two components:

1. Your relationship with the perpetrator,
2. Your relationship with yourself [9].

With regards to the latter, if you go into Victim and put the perpetrator into Persecutor, in other words if you go into drama about whatever took place, forgiveness is impossible. **To release yourself from an injustice, get out of drama first**.

Persecutors, many of you find it fun to beat up on a Victim. Maybe you get a little tickle of pleasure from it – some people get a lot.

But here's the deal - you know the switch is coming; when one of the other positions is about to clobber you and you get to be a Victim.

So how about this: instead of all that life energy expenditure in the Persecutor position, focused on the Victim and hoping to get something from that person – put your energy into figuring out what it is **you** really want and how to get it without the discounts.

Like I said in previous chapters, the justice system is full of Persecutors who became Victims after the switch. Divorce courts are full of Victims and Persecutors switching around like musical chairs. Quit the fault finding and look inside for what you want and how to problem solve for it.

Here are some Tips About Stopping Yourself from Discounting:

- **Listen to what people say and pay attention to how they finish their sentences:** with periods or question marks. Answer real questions, those with question marks, only if you want to. It's a discount to finish a person's sentence, even if they're 'floundering' around searching for a word or idea. The Victim might even say out loud, "What's the word I'm looking for?" It's not really a question posed to you. It could be an invitation to discount them. If you supply a word or finish their sentence, you've colluded with them in the discount. You've given them the message, 'yes you are incapable of, or too stupid to finish your sentence so I will do it for you.'

- If you absolutely cannot keep your mouth shut, when someone won't finish a sentence or when they won't ask explicitly for what it is they want, here's what to do - reflect back what you're observing (this is called *active listening*, which you'll learn in the next section). For example: "I'm hearing you wondering what word to use."

I invite you to think about why you are compelled to say anything while that person ponders a word selection. What's going on with you, that you must say something? What's your need that you hope will be satisfied by supplying the word? There we go, back to the last chapter.

- It's usually a discount to infer a request or a question from a statement. *For example,* a Victim might say, "I sure would like some eggs for lunch. I can't cook eggs. I always wreck them. You really know how to cook eggs." And if you respond to that, you're into drama. First notice that there are no question marks, so these aren't questions. You've participated in the discount that is: this person cannot ask straight out, "Will you cook me some eggs for lunch?" You've also reinforced a discount that the person wrecks eggs. The Rescuer's covert discounting message is something like, "Ah poor dear, you're too stupid to ask directly for what you want, and you're too clumsy to actually cook eggs, and too stupid to learn how, so I'll do the eggs." From the Persecutor position the discount would be overt, as in, "Can't form simple requests and I've seen what you do to eggs. It's egg-abuse. There otta be a law against it!"

A non-drama alternative is active listening: "I hear you say you like eggs and want eggs for lunch." Another option to drama is a question: "Are you asking for something?"

- Some people put on the Victim hat when they approach the refrigerator or cupboard looking for something to eat. "Mom, there's nothing to eat in here!" Notice again, there is no question mark at the end of that sentence. When someone is either covertly or blatantly hinting at a want, they're inviting you to infer a question, and then answer it. Ideally you say nothing or just reflect it back. Optionally, you can say, "Is there a request in there somewhere?" Another option is: "What's your question?" Another option is: "What do you need from me?" Notice that these are questions inviting the person to be present, to think, and to ask for what they want. A Victim will not give you an honest answer; because the purpose of the exchange isn't to solve a problem such as eating. The purpose of the exchange is to get into drama for the reasons we talked about in the last chapter.

- If you hear yourself explaining something to someone who hasn't explicitly asked for the explanation, you're probably discounting! You might think you're being helpful or even kind; but you don't know that, because the person hasn't asked for that. Your covert message may imply (what a Persecutor would say overtly), "Well, I know how this works, here let me say it so even a dummy like you can understand it." In some cultures, men consider themselves to be Mr. Fixit type Rescuers. So if a woman in that culture wants to share her feelings about something, for example sadness, with a Mr. Fixit, he'll suggest a 'solution' to her problem of sadness. Did she ask for a solution? No! So, if you're a Mr. or Mrs. Fixit – stop with the solutions till you hear a clear request. Likewise if a Mr. or Mrs. Fixit starts blabbing a solution to your self-disclosure, gently confront that discount with, "Ah, yes well, I want you to simply listen, not offer solutions. Are you willing to do that?"

When I was in grade school here in Canada back in the 60s, we kids had a special way of signaling to the teacher that we were excited about knowing an answer to her questions posed to the class. Suppose she asked, "Who knows where the

65

capital city of the United States is?" Well those of us who knew would throw our hands into the air, and then pump them up and down as if throwing wads of paper into the air. The harder we threw our hands up, the more excited we were about wanting to be called on to answer the question.

So too when you give advice, information, or an explanation to someone who hasn't asked for it, the motive may be to express enthusiasm, not get into drama. Likewise, when you receive advice, or an explanation, or information when you haven't asked for it, and/or don't want it, the other person's reason may be to express excitement and not discount. Unless the motivation is "listen to me, listen to me, I'm more important than you cause I know more." In which case a discount is going on and drama is starting up.

- Here's an example of a discount that gets played out in counseling rooms around the world. During a session with a counselor, the client begins to cry. As the tears flow down his or her face the counselor reaches to the tissue box and offers either the box or a tissue itself to the client. The covert message is, "You aren't capable of knowing that you have tears on your face, or maybe you don't know the rule about when to use a tissue for tears on your face; so I'll tell you. Nor are you capable of seeing tissues sitting on the table in front or beside you, so I'll supply them. Poor helpless you." If you're a counselor who does this tissue thing and you hear yourself protesting the example with words such as, "I'm only trying to help," I invite you to consider what needs of yours you are satisfying. For example, "I feel like I'm an unhelpful counselor over here while you cry; so I'll take care of my need to be helpful by doing something for you." And consider too that the client may interpret your tissue offer as a message that you think tears or feelings are unacceptable. "Here's a tissue to get those disgusting tears off your face. Now stop that crying!"

At a training event recently I had the opportunity to watch a room of about 70 therapists react to one individual expressing grief. Sobbing, moaning, shaking in a fetal position on the floor in front of her seat, this person was invited by the leader to come to the front and participate in a demonstration piece of therapy (clearing). The person began to crawl forward. I could see therapists around the room reveal their various levels of clinical wisdom by how they responded to this scene. Therapists who understood the necessity of self-activation made no move to assist. Less experienced therapists such as trainees either made a move to help, or displayed overt agitation & discomfort. The leader directed us to give her the dignity of asking for any help she needed rather than rescue her. The woman then actually asked for help standing up, and walked to the front on her own.

One more time – here's the attitude change required to stop discounting:

That person in agony on their death bed deserves the dignity of being a self-determining, self-directing human being - someone who can still decide what's best for themselves, even in a dire situation. It means they take responsibility for their experience of life, in the present, perhaps after a lifetime of Victimhood.

Here in the closing scene, they can choose to acknowledge their personal power, change their script, actually author the last sentence of the last paragraph of the last chapter without a whiney poor-me soundtrack.

Would you deny them the ultimate opportunity to look you in the eye and ask for what they want?

Set Clear Contracts and Boundaries to Discourage Others From Discounting You

If someone wants to discount you, there's no absolute method to prevent them from saying the words or taking the action other than complete physical restriction, which is unreasonable for most of us. However, having boundaries and contracts will inhibit potential discounts from a huge percent of possible opportunities.

Let's start with contracts, since I think they're easier to understand.

Contracts.

For our purposes here, a contract is an agreement established between two or more parties; where the parties can be people, groups, or parts of oneself.

The contract is made with enough detail so that all parties know what is expected of each other. It often has conflict resolution processes included so that in case of unforeseen deficits, a procedure is already in place for problem solving.

And often, when deliverables are involved, both positive and negative consequences are agreed on as well. In best case situations, the contract is explicit – all aspects are described. But in our daily social lives, many contracts are implicit if we are even aware of them at all. And this is where most people who want to get involved with drama have their chance.

Explicit social contracts include the laws that comprise the community in which we occupy physical space. Typical explicit social contracts deal with behaviors defined as criminal or dangerous, deviant or unjust, immoral or unethical. They have consequences we are all aware of. Contravention of an explicit social contract ideally results in the agreed on consequence. People who have the desire to get into a 3rd degree drama will know about the consequences because they are explicit.

Implicit social contracts on the other hand are nebulous. Children, immigrants, visitors and tourists to a culture will often contravene implicit social contracts until they learn through negative consequences what the contracts are. Staring at disfigured cripples is an implicitly forbidden activity in some cultures. Passing gas in an elevator is forbidden by an implicit social contract in my family culture. Not using certain words, such as 'fart', in certain or all social situations is also an implicit social contract in my family. Swear words are another example of vocabulary prohibited by implicit social contracts. Political correctness is an implicit social contract until it gets codified; making it explicit.

Implicit social contracts are full of potential dramatic opportunities simply because they are not fully explicit.

As a boy, I remember the drama I and my friends had with our grade five teacher when we discovered the dual meaning of the word 'cock'. To hear us talk in class you'd have thought we all had chicken coops. We were learning the vagaries of the implicit vocabulary social contract. And more importantly, we were learning how to invite someone into drama as Persecutor.

Suppose Mr. F. Ucker uses an implicitly banned word in the applicable context and situation. The volunteer enforcer of the contract, Mr. Prim N. Proper rescues the contract and everyone who read/heard the word by confronting Mr. F. Ucker as a Persecutor. In doing so, Mr. Proper thereby becomes the Rescuer. At that point, if Mr. Ucker wants to exchange strokes to bolster his stroke economy, he will either stay on the Persecutor position and continue discounting the contract with a further proliferation of expletives; or execute the switch to Victim claiming a 'poor me' of some kind, such as unjust accusation and misunderstanding, or simple innocence by way of impediment (such as incompetent parenting).

Alternatively, if Mr. F. Ucker was ignorant of the implicit social contract banning the word in question, and had no desire to get into drama, then a series of data gathering questions posed to Rescuer Mr. Prim N. Proper could lead to Mr. F. Ucker's apology and change in behavior (perhaps a name change from Mr. F. Ucker to just Mr. Ucker would be appropriate for the social contract) and bring the sequence to a quick halt before any intense, 3rd degree dramatic strokes are exchanged.

This remedial course of action illustrates how data gathering and dialogue can...

1. make implicit contracts explicit
2. can invite people into choosing to agree or not with the explicated contract
3. initiate new contracting

All of which reduce the potential for drama.

In homes where the family culture's code of behaviors and responsibilities are explicitly clear and agreed on, and both positive and negative consequences for keeping or breaking the agreements are easily described and evaluated, drama is greatly reduced. Just as in the workplace where job descriptions, performance expectations, and periodic evaluations are explicitly agreed on, the opportunities for people to jump into drama are significantly reduced.

The take home lesson here is this: establish clearly explicit contracts and you'll lower the probability of drama.

Social contracts aren't completely sufficient to prevent someone from discounting you. You also need clear boundaries.

Boundaries

Go back in time to science class when you first heard about cells. Maybe it was plant cells or maybe it was animal cells; but probably one of the facts you remember well is that every cell has a membrane around it. This cell membrane holds the cell together as a little unit. The cell membrane also acts as a boundary between the cell's insides and the outside environment. The cell membrane can allow some transport of 'things' in and out of the cell; and yet, for the cell to survive, the membrane acts as a filter. It literally defines where the cell begins and ends, and what can come in or go out.

People have psychological boundaries just like cell membranes. Our boundaries help define who we are, keep us enclosed psychologically, differentiate us from a surrounding environment, especially other people, and help decide what goes out, as in self-disclosure, and what comes in, as in listening to other people's descriptions of us.

Boundaries are, ideally, formed throughout childhood and into early adulthood. The idea of 'knowing yourself' has to do with boundaries.

Here are some basic boundary questions we ask ourselves in childhood:

- Where do I start and where do I end?
- How am I different from mommy?
- How am I different from daddy?
- Who will I allow to touch me?
- Who do I trust?
- What do I like to experience?
- Can I show myself to the world or do I have to hide from the world?

Obviously, boundaries are very important for getting along in the social reality. Too impenetrable and they become walls separating us from others; too porous and we lose touch with our individuality, blending into a collective. If you're a *Star Trek* fan, think of the boundary-less-ness of The Borg. Many mental health challenges arise from either of these extremes.

The social contracts we talked about earlier help us construct boundaries. Explicit contracting continues that process, and in this section we come a little closer in by detailing healthy boundaries. Knowing your boundaries helps you determine what you want, and what questions to ask – the conditions required to reduce or eliminate discounting.

The following list is a boundary setting inventory. The word 'right' is used with a meaning of ethical principle not as a claim of due. Starting with this phrase, 'Within the social contracts I've agreed to,' say the following to yourself...

- I have the right to all the wonderful times I have ever longed for in my life.
- I have the right to have joy in this life, to my space and quiet times, to relax, have fun right here right now.
- I have the right to be me, to love myself, to develop myself as a whole person, to carve out my place in this world.
- I have the right to reach out and ask for help, to go to places and seek out situations which will help me achieve my goals.
- I have the right to a sane, healthy way of life, to take calculated risks, to experiment with new strategies.
- I have the right to choose... to respond or not to respond... to be right... to be wrong... to disappoint myself... to change my mind ... to make mistakes and mess up...to miss the mark and blow it... to decide for myself... to decide not to decide.
- I have the right to leave or avoid people who manipulate me, humiliate me, discount me.
- I have the right to confront any behavior that is abusive or "crazy making".
- I have the right to trust my feelings, my hunches, my judgments, my intuition, to deviate in part or in whole from my parents' philosophy of life.
- I have the right to challenge and sort out the beliefs and ideas I was taught as a child, to keep what I want, to reject what I don't want.

71

- I have the right to as much time as I need - to gather any new information, to initiate changes in my life.
- I have the right to apply all the above now - not to wait until my family seeks help, gets well, gets happy, admits there is a problem.
- I have the right to feel, to think, to want, to imagine.
- I have the right to accept consequences.
- I have the right to fill my need to be touched, stroked, hugged, embraced, cuddled, caressed, held, and to determine when, where, how and who I want this with.
- I acknowledge your right to determine your physical boundary.
- I have the right to an exciting, satisfying, enjoyable, pleasurable sex life - to determine when, where, how and who I want this with.
- I acknowledge your right to determine your sexual boundary.
- I acknowledge that unless you have offended me in some major way, what I feel in response to your behavior is very often more about me and my history than about you (& visa-versa).
- I accept the responsibility to be aware of the impact my feelings have on you. I do not accept the responsibility how you feel and respond.
- I have the right to a vibrant, stimulating, healthy mental life and to my own thoughts.
- I acknowledge your right to your thoughts.
- I have the right to experience the full range of my feelings.
- I acknowledge your right to feelings.
- I have the right to explore the realms of the spirit and to choose my own concept of God or a Higher Power.
- I acknowledge your right to yours.
- I have the right to say yes.
- I have the right to say no!

The Hard Boundary - Saying No

In many families, part of the social contract is this: "You're not allowed to say no", or "Saying no is reserved for us parents".

As such, many people either cannot comfortably say no or cannot comfortably say no to parents and parent-like figures. I see this all the time in my psychotherapy practice, and in my opinion saying no with ease is the most important boundary building block to keep us drama free.

For example, Clara is a 58-year-old mother of two mid-twenties sons. Clara's mother Ruth is 75. The sons are forbidden by the implicit family social contract from saying no to Clara, who in turn is forbidden from saying no to Ruth.

Clara had, over the years, figured out indirect and, what we call, crooked (dishonest) ways of saying no without actually saying it. She was a master of excuses and lies; and in some cases making herself ill in order to implicitly say no. As Clara worked with me on this in therapy, she recognized how she used the same strategies with her husband, her friends, and her employer. She was able to see that her husband and sons used the same strategies too. Not saying no directly and explicitly was a family culture problem that created all sorts of drama and consequences.

So Clara began to use the phrases you'll be reading shortly, to say no to Ruth (such as "Ruth, that doesn't work for me."). Breaking such a contract is usually noticed by the parties involved, and of course Ruth picked up on it right away and confronted Clara for 'breach of contract'. Ruth called it disrespect. Clara's husband and sons also noticed the infraction; but because it wasn't with them, they simply observed.

Here's the sweet part – as Clara successfully survived the contract breaking with Ruth, Clara's husband and sons began experimenting with saying no explicitly as well, first with Clara, and then with each other.

As this honesty became 'normal' in the family, Clara implemented it with friends and her employer – and nothing bad happened! In fact, just the opposite took place, less drama all around. The only person who continued to protest the demise of the old contract was Ruth, who at last report was angry with her daughter's disobedience and insolence, blaming me, the therapist for Clara's ruination.

Do you see the new drama triangle Ruth set up? She was the Victim and I was the Persecutor (in absentia).

If someone is used to getting compliance from you by means of a contract that prohibits you from saying no, that person will react to hearing a no. So when you say no honestly and directly, be prepared for people to have a feeling response to this radical contract breaking behavior.

These folks will jump into drama in their favorite position and attempt to get you involved, with the goal of restoring the status quo – you, prohibited from saying no.

If their favorite position is Persecutor, you'll be invited to be Victim by way of insults, accusations, attacks and discounts. If their favorite position is Victim, you'll be invited to play Persecutor by way of accounts how hard done by they are as a result of your unfair, unloving, selfish, rude behavior. If their favorite position is Rescuer, you'll be invited to play Victim by way of seemingly intimate and nurturing concerned inquiries into what's going on that you'd act so selfishly.

If you have a religious and/or spiritual life, you could experience the person using it in their invitation to get you into drama. I'll use Christian in this example but it could be any practice or faith. The Persecutor for example might accuse you, "How can you call yourself a Christian?" The Victim might cry, "I thought you were a Christian." And the Rescuer might inquire, "What happened to your faith? This isn't how a Christian behaves."

Stand firm. You have the right to say no. All the great spiritual teachers and prophets said no, loud and clear. Do not <u>discuss</u> your decision without careful assessment of why you're discussing it; because most often the discussion is just part of the drama, with you being the Victim and the questioner being the Persecutor. Discussing it will be part of the implicit contract too as in, "The person who can out-debate the other, wins compliance."

I talk more about this in the section on asking for what you want.

How To Give a Clear Unconditional No

- No. That doesn't work for me.
- No thanks.
- I think I'll say no to that.
- Nope. Doesn't fit with me.
- Hmmm, I'll pass on that.
- I'm gonna pass that by.

- Not right now.
- Not interested.
- No I'm not gonna do that.
- I'm not willing to listen to you while you're yelling at me. Let me know when you want to talk.
- If you assault me, I'm calling the cops. You'll be arrested. It's that simple.

The Gas Woman Story: So one fine spring day I was washing my motorbike in the driveway when a young woman walked off the sidewalk and approached me. She was well dressed and groomed, displaying an official type name badge and carrying a clipboard with a sheaf of papers. I smelled door-to-door sales perfume immediately.

She: "Good day sir. Nice day for biking."

Me: "Yep."

She: "I'm with Official Sounding Gas Company, and we're checking your neighborhood to ensure taxpayers are paying appropriate prices for natural gas. May I see a recent gas utility bill?"

Me: "No."

She: "Well it will only take a moment and we're confirming that the pricing structure is in compliance with regional standards; so I'll need to see a recent gas invoice."

Me: "I'm not going to show you."

She: "I'm authorized by Official Sounding Gas Company to review your bill as part of a national price compliance initiative."

Me: "I'm not going to show you."

She: "Your gas company may be in violation of pricing mandates."

Me: "I'm not showing you."

She: "You may be paying too much for your gas."

Me: "I'm not showing you."

She: "You don't care if you're paying too much?"

Me: "I'm not showing you."

She: ... <pause> ... "Must be nice having all the money you want."

Me: <silent>

She: ... <walks away> ...

In this Gas Woman scenario, I said no to her request. Then she switched to making statements that implied the original request was still unanswered, a discount to me. Notice that her second statement was when she got into Drama in the Rescuer position with the one-up ulterior transaction, 'I'm here to help ignorant consumers, of which you may be one.'

I switched to a stronger version of saying no. Then I used what's called the broken record method of just repeating that phrase for each of her remaining statements.

Actually, none of these follow up statements were questions so I didn't need to respond at all. I refused to get dramatic with her, despite her repeated attempts to convince me I might be a Victim.

Her final transaction was when she switched positions to Victim by putting me in a one-up position of having all the money I want. She did this in her mind, not with me in reality because I didn't respond.

This is another example how a person can be in a drama by themselves as in Sample 5 from previous chapters.

How To Give a Softer or Conditional No

- Now's not a good time, ask me *<specific time or date>*.
- I'm not willing to do that until *<specify the conditions>*
- I'm not that interested, but I want more details before I definitely say yes or no.
- That's an interesting proposal. I'll think about it and get back to you by *<specific time or date>*.
- I like your idea; except for the part about ... How about this as an option?
- I'm willing to give you a definite maybe. When do you need an answer?
- Any wiggle room in your request? *Yes*: Great, when should I get back to you by? *No*: Well thanks for thinking of me, I'll pass this time.
- Hmmm, my quick response is a no; but here's my concern ... Any ideas how I might problem solve these?
- I'd like to think of myself as an expert on that subject; but realistically I'm not the person to respond to that.
- I hear that you're furious with me. I'm willing to work this out with you when you're not so mad. Will you let me know when that is?

- I can see that you're having a strong reaction to this. Let me know when you think we can problem solve it.
- I'm very upset with what you just said/did. I need to calm myself before we discuss it further. I'll get back to you by *<specific time or date>*.
- This issue has a long history between us so I'm not willing to discuss it further until I/we get some counseling.
- I hear that you're upset with me about saying no, and I don't like to see you having these feelings so when you think of another option or variation on your request I'll definitely listen to it.

Boundaries - Tips

If a Victim invites you into drama, here are some powerful boundary creating statements:

- I hear that you're upset. I'm not an expert on this so I'm not going to insult your intelligence and capabilities with advice. I know you can find the answers to this.
- The picture you describe sounds bleak. I have faith that you'll figure it out.
- I remember when you faced *<give example of a previous challenge>*. I'm confident you can prevail through this too.

If a Rescuer invites you into drama with advice, here are some powerful boundary creating statements:

- I know you mean well; but what I need is someone willing to just listen. I've seen you do that really well in the past. Are you willing to just listen again?
- Hmmm, I can tell that you're interested in helping and I appreciate that. However, I'm not wanting advice just now.
- I know your heart's in the right place; but I'm actually not asking for ideas.

To set boundaries with anyone, including drama Persecutors here's the four components you need to implement:

i.   Identify and state the discounting behavior to the person *i.e. When you offer me a beer even though I've said no thanks ...*

ii.   State your emotional response i.e. *I feel disrespected.*

iii.   Demand the behavior change that acknowledges your boundary i.e. *I'm not going to accept a drink from you so stop offering.*

iv.   Have a backup plan if the demand is ignored i.e. *leave, stronger confrontation about the behavior, call on external structures for support (ie. employer, lawyer, police).*

Imagine a small acorn that has just sprouted and is a little sapling. Now imagine a full grown oak tree.

Which is easier to pull out?

Same with discounts – catch the first ones – do not let them grow. Do not ignore them with excuses like needing to be polite, or not wanting to cause a scene.

If a Persecutor invites you into drama with overt discounts, here are some powerful boundary creating statements:

- I'm not willing to fight with you even if you insult me, are critical, or condescending.
- I'm not willing to agree with you.
- I can see how you'd think I'm *<something bad>*; and I'm not going to change my mind.
- Hmmm, yes I *<did or said whatever>*. Here's what I'll do differently next time.
- Hmmm, yes I *<made that mistake>*. What's your preference for next time?
- Ok, yes I *<did or said whatever>*. What's your request?
- Well, we share a difference about that.
- Isn't it amazing how two people can have such different views of the same thing; yet still respect each other?
- Specifically, what behaviors are you asking me to change?

Boundaries – The Subtle Power of Active Listening

Imagine a frenetic talker doing a rant at you. Picture the words slicing through space in your direction like photon torpedoes. Imagine the energy coming your way. If you put up hard shields hoping to defend yourself by blocking the energy, you'd better put as much energy into your shields as is coming your way.

That could get tiresome, especially if the other person has a gunnysack discharging at you. On the other hand, if you had shields that could flex and bend with the energy like a blade of grass in a tornado, you would have little effort expenditure.

Active listening is a method of listening to someone without absorbing their energy. It's a bending and moving in harmony with the other's flow; yet maintaining integrity of self-identity. In other words, you can maintain boundaries with minimal effort.

The bonus feature of active listening is that the talker does not feel resistance. When a person who is self-disclosing feels resistance, s/he will usually increase the energy output in order to overpower it - in order to be heard – in order to get some respect (to be noticed).

This is usually in the form of volume. Ever observed an argument escalate into a shouting match? That's because neither person feels heard so they turn up the energy i.e. volume.

With active listening, the talker absolutely knows the listener is present, and more importantly – listening.

The talker has no need to increase energy output. Active listening is also called reflective listening; but I'm not a fan of that term because it's been misunderstood to mean parroting. Picture a parrot mimicking someone. The bird has no understanding of what the communication intends to mean. Active listening, in stark contrast, strives to reflect back the meaning of the talker's self-disclosure.

Active listening is conducted by the person who is listening to a talker. The talker self-discloses. The listener does both listening and talking; but the listener's talking part is *not self-disclosure.*

Here's a sample, and I recommend that you read it two or three times:

Barbara: "I've been thinking about our trip to Vancouver and wondering what to wear when we go hiking. It could be cool down by the ocean but hot over by your sister's place."
Greg: "You're wondering how to dress for hiking."

Barbara: "And the chance of rain. It's often days of drizzle with short hot spells."

Greg: "What to do about rain gear."

Barbara: "Exactly. It seems like overkill to pack everything for just a long weekend."

Greg: "Short trip, big suitcase."

Barbara: "Ok, I've decided. Talking with you helped. I'm taking everything I might need."

In this snippet, Barbara starts the conversation, so she's the talker and thus the self-discloser. I'm the listener – the active listener.

I listen to what she says, then I say the content back in my own way.

Can you see in this sample how Barbara knows that she is being heard?

And notice too in the example that I don't self-disclose my thoughts about what she's saying. I've decided that this is her time to talk, not mine. Thus, I have boundaries.

If I choose to self-disclose my thoughts and plans or whatever, I'll do so after she is completely finished. Or I may choose not to – again, that's boundary setting. I often choose not to self-disclose in order to have boundaries; keeping my thoughts to myself.

Ok, so that's one version of active listening. A more powerful and sophisticated version is to listen for feelings as well as content; and say them back to the talker.

The reason for reflecting back feelings is that sometimes we can't fully relate to each other on a content level.

For example, when a woman talks about childbirth, few if any men can relate. But if she talks about her feelings concerning child birth, such as excitement and fear, males can relate because they know about excitement and fear.

Another example is if I start talking about my piloting experiences spinning a single engine aircraft, non-pilots have trouble relating. But when I include how much fun it was after the terror of the first few spins, most people understand what I'm talking about because they've experienced terror, and/or fun, and maybe in that order.

We relate to each other, we understand each other, based on feelings. We experience other people as similar to ourselves using feelings as a commonality.

This version of active listening is called **empathic listening**. As listeners we're after empathy. Not sympathy, which is feeling the same feelings at the same time.

When we're in sympathy with another person we're feeling what the other is feeling at the same time i.e. crying together.

We can theoretically relate to another person who is feeling what we are; but in practice we don't do it very well because we're not listening. Instead, we're self-disclosing sympathetically. So now we've got two self-disclosers.

Remember what happens when two self-disclosers get going? *Neither one feels heard so they turn up the volume!*

So in empathic listening we don't want to <u>have</u> the same feeling experience as the talker. But we do want to know what feelings the person is self-disclosing, and say them back in our own words.

Here's a sample:

Barbara: "I'm quite excited to see my brother. Just two more days and we're there."
Greg: "Enjoying the trip already?"
Barbara: "Yep, isn't that what you used to say, the experience starts with the planning. I always enjoy the buildup to a trip."
Greg: "Fun getting ready."
Barbara: "And a little sad, I wish we could visit more often."
Greg: "And you're in touch with how much he means to you."
Barbara: "I do love him."

When a person is self-disclosing feelings, and a listener reflects the understanding of those feelings, the self-discloser knows they've been emotionally heard. The self-discloser experiences a satisfaction with the communication because it has succeeded.

The whole point of talking is to be understood. The whole point of listening is to understand.

In the next chapter I'm bringing back the samples we saw in chapters One and Two, and in some of those samples you'll see more active listening.

Ask For What You Want in an Honest Way (and have backup plans).

People have the ability to ask for what they want, from as many sources and as often as necessary until they solve the want.

House pets such as dogs and cats make their needs known to us. They don't need drama to do so. Kitty wants a pet, what does she do? She rubs against your leg. Pooch wants a pet, what does he do? He sits in front of you, jumps up on your chest, barks, or fetches your slippers. If animals can figure out what they want and how to ask for it, people can as well.

The drama free behavior is, 'Ask for what you want in an honest way (and have backup plans).' This is similar to contracting; where you build an explicit contract with another person to get your needs met.

Sounds easy when you read that, doesn't it?

Trick is, when we were children, we did ask, and (for most of us) what we got instead was a harsh lesson of some kind promoting the message, 'don't ask for what you want.' Some of us only needed one lesson to get the message. Some of us used repeated lessons until we got the learning. At some defining moment, we got zapped emotionally and 'learned our lesson'.

The methods by which caregivers transmit the 'don't ask' message are extensive. Each ethnic and family culture has an influence on a caregiver's unique way of conveying it.

In Roger's family, as an example, asking for a stroke such as, "Do you love me?" was strictly forbidden. In fact, he doesn't recall ever seeing his parents show affection even for each other. As such, strokes were tokenized into material goods and services, To express love and care, they gave each other goods and services.

If Roger wanted a stroke, he tokenized it into some physical item like new skates. He was expected to compile a set of reasons why he wanted the skates. He'd present the persuasive argument to his father who would engage him in an oral exam of sorts on the validity of each reason. I call this the **Debate Society** (see below). Unfortunately for Roger, he was a child, unfamiliar with multi-media sales presentations or power point, and was rarely able to legitimize his wants and out-debate father. Roger grew up feeling inadequate and deprived most of the time.

Only when father approved of Roger's request, would Roger get what he wanted, which was in fact what father wanted him to get, making it more of father's want, not Roger's. Father would even 'talk Roger out of' what he wanted in a reverse take-over procedure and convince Roger to accept what father thought he should have.

By the time Roger was a teen, he hardly knew what he wanted about anything because the anxiety of preparing justification for the subsequent inquiry was a zapper, killing the desire before he was fully aware of it. As such, Roger was in a constant state of stroke deprivation.

And guess how compelling drama was to satisfy that need?

As another example of how caregivers convey the message 'don't ask for what you want', I'll switch focus to Bill and his mother. Bill's nurturing needs were tokenized into services with her, such as making meals. What he observed when he asked for something from her was either an extreme emotional event, such as threat of suicide; or a detached and cold, incomplete unsatisfying service delivery. Both of these responses acted as negative reinforcement for asking what he wanted, leaving Bill stroke deprived. And guess how compelling the drama was to satisfy that need?

Both these people experienced family cultures that promoted drama rather than honest requests for needs and wants.

At the same time we're getting that 'don't ask for what you want' message, the grownups around us are demonstrating the acceptable ways needs and wants can be fulfilled; which always includes drama, and specifically the family or culture approved dramatic position.

So in these client's families, for example, Roger and Bill learned that the approved position on the drama triangle to get stroke needs met was to be a Rescuer.

In fact, all the men on both sides of their family trees going back in history were accomplished Rescuers. Where there's a Rescuer there has to be a Victim; and since the men were Knights in Shining Armor, the women were Damsels in Distress. Father played the Knight, mother played the Damsel, Roger and Bill played Young Knights in Training.

When I presented these clients with the material you're reading here, it was as if foggy glasses came off, and they each understood for the first time the actual dynamics of the more dramatic transactions they'd experienced for years in their families of origin, and in their current families.

Mothers, aunts, step-mothers, mothers-in-law, sisters, sisters-in-law, ex-wives, wives and daughters were all Victims.

Fathers, uncles, step-fathers, fathers-in-law, brothers-in-law, brothers and sons were all Rescuers in an endless convoluted dramatic stage play.

Watch any daytime 'soap opera' and you'll see family type drama triangles all over the place.

With that background, let's shift now to the methodology of asking for what you want or need.

The most powerful phrases for initiating requests that I've discovered after almost thirty years of research and teaching this are the following:

- Will you *<specific need or want>*?
- Are you willing to *<specific need or want>*?
- When will you *<specific need or want>*?
- What do you think of the idea that you *<specific need or want>*?
- Do you have some ideas about how I can *<specific need or want>*?
- Ok, so I need to confirm for myself that you'll *<specific action/behavior>*. Is that right?

Some simple examples of *<specific need or want>* that clients typically report to me are:

- Household responsibilities, such as clear the table, wash the dishes, make dinner, make your own lunch, add to the grocery list, buy the groceries, fill the car with gas, take out the trash etc..
- Problem solve *<whatever – ie. Vacation planning, budgeting, disruptive behavior>* with me/us.
- Accept responsibility for a task.

Here are a few examples of *<the specific need or want is for strokes>*:

- Give me a hug.
- Share a hug.
- Tell me you love me.
- Tell me what you like about my *<accomplishment, appearance, completed task>*.
- Tell me you appreciate *<what I just did>*.
- Buy me a souvenir on your trip.
- Phone me when you get there.
- Wait for me at the finish line.

Putting some of these together then we get the following examples of complete requests:

- ✓ Will you clear the table?
- ✓ When will you do the dishes?
- ✓ Ok, so I need to confirm for myself that you'll clear the table and do the dishes. Is that right?
- ✓ Bob, will you check tickets at the door?
- ✓ What do you think of the idea that you buy me a souvenir on your trip?
- ✓ Are you willing to call me each night while you're away?
- ✓ Will you give me a hug?
- ✓ Will you share a hug?
- ✓ I need to confirm for myself that even when I make mistakes you still love me. Is that right?

The expression of a want or need is <u>not</u> a request.

For example, saying "I need a hug," is not a request. It is only a statement of need. The request is 'Will you give me a hug?' Likewise, making a general announcement of a need such as, "I need someone

85

to check tickets at the door," is not a request; it's just a statement of a need. The request is 'Bob, will you check tickets at the door?'

The statement 'I don't feel you love me' is a disclosure of inner experience, not a request for anything; so if someone says that to you, don't start a rescue mission. Wait for an explicit request, otherwise you're in drama - besides which, making someone feel loved is out of your control.

A request to you would be 'Will you tell me something you love about me?'

The statement 'You don't make me happy anymore' is another self-disclosure, not a request. Don't touch it or you'll be in drama. A request to you would be 'Are you willing to set up a weekly date night with me, just the two of us, so we can connect like we used to?'

Because the exchange of strokes is so rewarding while in drama, people around you will continue to get dramatic in an attempt to get their stoke needs met.

This can be tiresome to say the least – constantly resisting drama invitations. People desperate for strokes will move into each position to issue an invitation to you: they will try it from the Victim with 'poor me' stories; they will attempt to help you solve a problem, putting you in a Victim one-down position so they can be Rescuer; or they will overtly discount or insult you from Persecutor, hoping you'll respond.

If you are not fully powered up on the strategies discussed so far, you may be vulnerable to one of these invitations.

Indeed, people will experiment with invitations to you in order to discover your particular vulnerability; which becomes their favorite way past your boundaries, getting you into drama. Technically we call this your **gimmick** and it's like a bait that you're susceptible to.

If fish knew they were 'fished' with worms, they would probably give them up. Indeed in many trout waters, the trout are 'educated' and will refuse to eat anything during daylight hours – when fishermen are active. Similarly, when you know what your bait, (your gimmick) is, you can avoid it.

Here's an example...

It is common in social groups for someone to 'make a joke' about or make fun of another; except it's not funny to the recipient.

This is actually an invitation from the initiating joke teller as Persecutor, to the recipient to get dramatic and exchange some negative strokes either as Victim or sharing the Persecutor position.

If Rescuers don't intervene and get into drama first, the recipient of the 'joke' probably will jump on. If this is into the Persecutor as a shared position, there will be a rebuttal insult or overt discount of the initiator. The initiator might respond, "Woa, easy now. Can't ya take a joke?" Again from the Persecutor position in an attempt to once more put the recipient into a one-down Victim position with the identified flaw of not being able to take a joke.

Persecution invitations like this are very alluring and perhaps experienced as demanding, and often will get us into drama in a battle for that Persecutor position - two people insulting each other until one person moves to Victim. Many 2nd degree dramas are verbal insult battles. Many 3rd degree dramas begin there, and end with actual fist fights to determine who will be the Victim.

The drama free tactic for the 'joke' recipient is to ask the Persecutor to state that it wasn't an insult, "Bob, I don't think that's funny. I'm hoping you didn't mean it to be an insult so will you tell me that wasn't your intent?" If Bob states that it was an insult, ask for an apology. If he refuses, go to active listening and problem solving with a question, "So you _are_ trying to insult me. What is it you want by doing that?"

The Debate Society

A common tactic of parents for child behavior management is the engagement of reasoning in the family culture contract. If a child can explain his reasons for thoughts, feelings, behaviors, needs/wants to the satisfaction of the inquiring parent, then the parent judges the thoughts, feelings, behaviors, needs/wants as valid.

Of course a child is usually intellectually overpowered by an adult so it's an 8 day week when a child can out-debate a parent. Children learn other ways, including drama to get their needs met[10].

The use of reason has its utility, no question; but each of us has a right to decide when that is. So if you don't want to discuss some thought, feeling, behavior, want/need, you can choose not to. The other person may decide to get into drama because their needs are not being met by reasoning – like when they were a child and lost the debate to daddy or mommy – so you should be ready for the invitations to get into drama.

In the Gas Woman story above, I refused to enter into any discussion. I expected the company she was representing had worked out all the arguments that a home owner might have to changing natural gas suppliers. The sales team probably had to memorize these and role play them until each sales person was adept at out-debating home owner resistance. The woman who approached me intended to recruit me into the debate society and then out-reason me! I refused to get involved. You can too.

Suppose someone you're close to, a friend for example, wants to get you to go along with something, and you don't want to. Perhaps you fear losing this person as a friend if you say no. Well **I invite you to consider that a friend you want in your life, is someone who will hear a no and respect it. A friend will want a win-win. A friend you can do without is a person who hears a no and doesn't respect it.**

Let's talk about family and saying no.

The heart of a functionally healthy family is the willingness of each member, of every member, to be concerned about the wellbeing of each other – mutually. What I hear over and over in my psychotherapy practice from clients is a family system that has a lop-sided concern for wellbeing; meaning someone's wellbeing gets lower priority, or sadly, no priority.

Frequently the reality is that the family is not conducting itself like a loving family. In such a family it makes sense that promoting your wellbeing as equally important to others, is a worthy initiative.

A key tactic for doing so is the ability to say no, and to not be 'talked out of it'. Do not join the debate society when the topic is the reduction of your wellbeing! Likewise, be vigilant for discounts to the wellbeing of other family members and refuse to participate.

If your family disowns you because you say no, is that the type of family you want?

And let's talk about a cultural mistaken belief we have here in Canada and the United States, and probably elsewhere, which concerns asking for what you want.

The mistaken belief goes like this: if you have to ask for it, its value diminishes.

Typically the belief is applied to strokes such as intimate moments, alone times, hugs, sex, confirmations of love, and gifts (that are tokens for these strokes). So, according to the mistaken belief, if I have to ask my wife for a hug, then the act of asking diminishes or eliminates the value of the hug.

What a crazy belief! Hey, when we go into a restaurant, we ask for a meal; and does the asking make it tasteless?

When we go to buy a pair of shoes, does the asking for what we want make them uncomfortable?

Only if you follow the belief.

This mistaken belief has an evil sibling: if a person really loves me I shouldn't have to ask for what I want. Which really means that the ability to mind read comes with truly loving someone.

That's ludicrous!

Here's how it starts though. As infants, unable to ask for what we wanted, such as a diaper change, other than by self-disclosure of discomfort, caregivers arrived at our crib-sides and delivered needs; often accompanied by touches, caresses, kisses, and soft vocalizations conveying love and care. We attached the expression of their love with the amazing ability to deliver our needs without us asking. We carry that early cognition forward in time to present day when we project it onto our spouse and say, "If he really loved me, he would know what I want!"

Can you imagine if getting a restaurant meal was contingent on the server calling someone who loved you and asking that person what meal you should be served?

<1970s telephone ring tone>

89

Mrs. Boyce:	"Hello"
Server:	"Ah, is this Mrs. Boyce?"
Mrs. Boyce:	"Yes, who's this?"
Server:	"This is Bill the Server at Risto Feasto Bistro."
Mrs. Boyce:	"I'm not interested in telemarketers. Good bye."

Server: "Wait wait Mrs. Boyce I have Greg Boyce, your son sitting here at table 21."

Mrs. Boyce: "Who's sitting there?"

Server: "Your son Greg Boyce; you know, psychotherapist, author, fly fisherman."

Mrs. Boyce: "He's at a restaurant? Why is he sitting at table 21?"

Server: "Ah, well, he'd like to enjoy one of our entrés. Our procedure here at Risto Feasto is to serve exceptional meals ordered by a patron's loved ones, since they know best what the patron really wants to eat. This will prove how much you love him."

Mrs. Boyce: "Oh my goodness, a test. <taking a breath> I'm ready."

Server: "Do you love Greg?"

Mrs. Boyce: "Of course, ever since he was a baby. He's always been a good boy, well, until he started to say no to me. It all started with that therapist teaching him to say no. Did I pass the test?"

Server: "Ah, it's a two part test, that was part one. Here's part two, since you love him, you'll know what he wants to eat from our exclusive executive chef menu?"

Mrs. Boyce: "I remember when he was in grade seven he wanted ring-tum-ditty every day for lunch. That went on for months. I'm sure he wants ring-tum-ditty."

Server: "I'm not familiar with that. Does ring-tum-ditty have any other names?"

Mrs. Boyce: "Stewed tomatoes and melted cheddar cheese poured over white buttered toast."

Server: "Thank you Mrs. Boyce. Chef will be happy to prepare ring-tum-ditty."

Mrs. Boyce: "Or liver & onions. He should have liver and onions once a week. Did you know liver is an excellent source of... "<interrupted>

Server: "Good bye Mrs. Boyce."

What we need to know is this: our caregivers paid attention to us, observed our need and wants, developed best guesses of our needs and wants and then delivered them based on those probabilities.

If changing the diaper didn't work to calm us down they switched to feeding; if that didn't work they switched to burping and walking around. And if that didn't work, they may have tried ring-tum-ditty.

No mind reading involved.

No cognitive upload from the feeling of love.

What really took place was observation, probabilities, and experimentation resulting in successful delivery of unarticulated wants.

Same thing today with your spouse – if he is observant of your expression of wants and needs and he experiments with delivery, then success goes up. The motive for this may be love; but love is not the tool.

Backup Plans (Options)

These terms refer to the idea of having another plan ready to go if your first plan doesn't succeed. It's commonly known as **having options**. At some point with almost all my clients the subject of backup plans is covered because of its importance.

Think of backup plans like insurance, a type of life insurance – insurance for a satisfying fulfilling life.

I've made it a regular practice in my life to have options. When I plan to go to a movie with a friend I figure out what I'll do if he cancels at the last minute. Rather than be disappointed, will I go solo or who can I call last minute?

When I plan on going fishing I decide on a couple of different places, in case water conditions are un-fishable.

When planning a vacation with my wife we think about options for all aspects of it, so that we never feel disappointed.

Naturally, planning like that takes mental, emotional, and physical energy; but the process gets easy with practice. The rewards are worth the effort – a satisfying life.

Chapter Summary

Victims:

Do you know what you want? Can you ask a question?

Good, read on.

1. Give yourself credit for all the talents, skills, capabilities, characteristics, qualities, and virtues that you have at your disposal for solving problems.
2. Stop discounting yourself.
3. Stop blaming and laying responsibility on others. It's your life – author it.
4. Problem-solve what you need and want (especially strokes); figure out a plan; figure out alternative backup plans.
5. Ask for what you want. Ask as often as you need to.
6. Identify contracts you're living in and evaluate if you want to keep them in place or not.
7. Set up contracts that support you.
8. Set boundaries. Respect others boundaries.

Persecutors:

1. Anytime you feel like criticizing someone, look at what you need or want and you're **not** asking for, <u>especially strokes</u>. Acting out, rebelliousness or oppositional defiance is very often done for strokes. If you escalate from a 1st degree to 2nd and/or to 3rd degree drama, then for sure you are stroke deprived. Figure out what you need to receive at a deep emotional place.
2. Stop persecuting and discounting others. Give them credit for all the talents, skills, capabilities, characteristics, qualities, and virtues that they have at their disposal for solving problems.
3. Problem-solve what you need and want; figure out a plan; figure out alternative backup plans.
4. Ask for what you want.
5. Set up contracts that support you.
6. Respect others boundaries. Set your own.

Rescuers:

1. Look at the Victim and ask yourself if the person is 'poor me' or not, in order to discern a Victim from a victim.
2. Anytime you feel like rescuing, look at what **you** need and aren't asking for, especially strokes.
3. Problem-solve what you need and want (especially strokes); figure out a plan; figure out alternative backup plans.
4. Ask for what you want.
5. Set up contracts that support you.
6. Respect others boundaries. Set them for yourself, especially if you work in a helping profession (or you'll burn out).

Last and Not Least

Picture yourself on a narrow trail through the thickest of Amazon rain forests. The foliage towers above you, obscuring a view of the sky; but shafts of misty sunlight slice down, kissing the verdant green understory. All around you is lush vibrancy. Unseen birds and countless insects sing and call in a cacophony of symphonies.

Abruptly all is quiet. The hair on the back of your neck stands up. You stop, feet frozen in place. The sudden silence is deafening. Your heart begins to pound, adrenaline shooting into every cell of your body as your instinct for survival is aroused.

You slowly turn and look behind. Crouching in the shadows just there on the back trail is a midnight black jaguar. Its piercing yellow eyes lock to yours. Its tail slowly moves in that particular manner of all stalking cats, just before they pounce for prey.

Every cell in your body tingles with electrifying clarity: the jaguar has decided this is a good time for dinner and you're the main course.

Are you insulted? Do you take this personally? Is this a statement specifically about you; or could the prey item be any warm blooded trail wanderer?

I invite you to conclude that in this scene you're a walking meal in the right place at the wrong time (from your point of view), and there's nothing personal about it.

It's not about **you**.

The jaguar is doing what a jaguar does, and you dear reader have very little to do with that, other than putting yourself in that location.

Same is true for many social interactions that you could take personally and be insulted or discounted by and hence jump into drama. In that moment, remember this story and it's not really about you, it's about the other person and their needs being achieved by whatever it is they're thinking, feeling, or doing.

Example: I once had a neighbor who was a professional Mr. Fixit. If he came outside and I was doing something, he had some 'good advice' to share with me about that something. Even in areas where I had expertise; he apparently had extra expertise. I could smell his odoriferous advice coming down the sidewalk all on its own before his arrival.

I took it personally for a bit; until I remembered the jaguar story. Thereafter I noticed he gave advice to everyone on the occasions I watched him. His behavior was actually all about him and very little to do with the rest of us. He probably would have offered boxing advice to Mohammed Ali back when, if given the opportunity. Like the jaguar, he was just doing what he did to get his needs met – inefficiently from the Rescuer position.

Since it actually did me no harm, I relaxed, and with that came an appreciation for the uniqueness of who he was, for the beauty of his human beingness and his desire to connect with people. And maybe, once a year, I learned something useful in addition.

Mission Possible

Pull out your drama sheet you've been building since chapter one. What's your favourite dramatic position? Are you willing to make the attitude change required to stop discounting? If yes, what skills, strengths and virtues do you have, to get on with your life? Are you willing to figure out what you want and what questions to ask to get what you want? Ok, do so.

Next up, a stroll down memory lane as we revisit the samples and see how to avoid drama.

Chapter 5

The Samples One More Time

Drama Free

In chapters one and two I presented some examples of drama. Let's go back through them one by one and look at how you could decline the invitations using what we know from the last chapter.

The attitude change we talked about is behind the scenes, whispering to us not to discount ourselves or others.

As a reminder while you read these samples - to detect an invitation for drama, be aware of:

o   'Poor me – I'm such a loser/mess/lost cause' type of message – this will be from a Victim.

o   'Poor you – I can help you' type of message – this is from a Rescuer. It can also be about another person as in, "I feel sorry for Greg. He's trying so hard to write a great chapter. What can we do to keep him from falling on his face?"

o   'You're such a loser' type of message – from a Persecutor. It can also be about another person, such as, "Greg is such an ego maniac. Who is he to write a book on drama."

To do this chapter, I'll again indent my comments in italics. Unlike the other times through the samples; the dramas will be short-lived because we refuse the invitations.

Sample 1: You and your friend Flora are at the local coffee shop visiting. Flora starts the sequence:

This example of drama we called 'Yes But'. That's from Flora's point of view. It was called 'I Was Only Trying To Help' from the listener or your point of view. Essentially it's about giving and receiving advice. This time through the sample you're not going to accept the invitation to play Rescuer to Flora's Victimhood.

Flora: "I just don't know what to do about Paul. He's so distracted by work these days that he never spends any time with us. I'm beginning to think he's a workaholic." <*Deep sigh*> "I'm really worried."

The opening sentence is a declaration of not knowing what to do about a situation, so it's not an overt self-discount; but the sigh is a give-away that Flora has taken the Victim position of 'poor me' with some kind of internal self-discount. By not making a request or a clear statement of purpose for what she wants from the disclosure she is inviting you to get into drama.

You: "Ah, you're concerned."

All you do is indicate you heard her. This is empathic listening, where you reflect back the feeling you hear. It's a stroke; but not much of one and not likely to reinforce her Victimhood. Your stance for this is the attitude that Flora has all that she needs to problem solve her marriage – the ability to know what she wants and the ability to ask questions. Notice that she's not asking you a question. She's making statements. Simply listening at this time is the way for you to be in relationship with Flora without discounting her.

Flora: "He won't even commit to a time when we can discuss it. He says it's all in my imagination."

But she goes ahead with her tale of woe as a Victim. Notice it's a simple self-disclosure statement, not a question, nor a request. It's not even a discount.

You: "You're saying he won't discuss your concerns."

More active listening. This is just telling her you're present. You're not stroking her Victimhood.

Flora: "I thought of counseling, but the counselor said Paul had to come in as well."

When a person doesn't get the strokes for Victim, sometimes they actually start to problem solve by talking through aspects of the situation.

You: "Yea that's a problem."

> *Again, just active listening – walking alongside Flora as she describes what's happening.*

Flora: <*weeping*> "I even tried the sexy approach. He hardly noticed. I feel worse now. I don't want to talk about this anymore."

> *Feeling worse is not necessarily a bad place to be, because as a result she may be motivated to problem solve rather than start drama. This is well known to therapists: feeling better is a result of problem solving, not being rescued. Not getting rescued, getting few strokes, Flora decides to stop the exchange. And very important to notice that she does this without a switch of positions – proof you were not in drama!*

You: <*quietly*> "I have confidence you'll figure out how to solve this like you did with your father's dementia."

> *This is a stroke for Flora's ability to solve problems. The evidence cannot be denied which makes it all the more powerful. It's a loving stroke, not a discount.*

Concluding this set of transactions, Flora still feels sad; which might be labeled as 'bad feelings'. But unlike the drama version, you have nothing to do with those feelings. Nor did you stroke her for being a Victim.

The fact you didn't participate in discounting her is of prime importance in this sample. Pat yourself on the back. The other thing to notice about this sample is the use of active listening to remain in relationship with Flora. Active listening, and its more powerful derivative, empathic listening, are excellent skills to acquire if you aren't well versed with them.

Sample 2: You and your buddy Paul are sipping beers and watching the game on a Saturday afternoon. It is halftime and you casually start a conversation about your motor bike.

> *The first time around, you were perceived as a Victim. From Paul's point of view we called this 'I Was Only Trying to Help' and from your point of view we called it 'Na, tried that, didn't work. What else ya got?' Like the previous sample, this is about advice giving and receiving – a rampant form of drama. This time through the sample however you will not support his attempt to invite you (covertly discount you) into Victim with a Rescue.*

You: "Yea, I was out on the bike last night."

A straight forward self-disclosure.

Paul: "Beauty of a night for it."

A clear statement of opinion.

You: "Woulda bin, but the bike was running rough and I didn't get far."

> *Another self-disclosure. Unlike the original sample, you add detail and are not 'baiting' him.*

Paul: "How come?"

> *Clear easy honest question of curiosity.*

You: "Yea, good question. You interested in thinking it through with me?

> *A very powerful transaction this one. Asking for collegial problem solving – as equals. No Victimhood here. An example of asking for what you want – contracting, that is founded on the attitude that you can know what you want and you can ask questions in order to figure out how to get what you want.*

Paul: "Ah, yea. I'm wondering about dirty gas."

> *Since most people aren't clear and straight, he's a little surprised at the honest request; but starts the problem solving.*

You: "I just filled up, and replaced both the gas and air filters, and the plugs a week ago. Do you think it could be dirty gas even so?"

> *Notice how you don't bat his suggestion back like a ping-pong ball? That could easily slide into 'yea but' and drama. Instead, you are doing research by providing data and asking a follow-up question.*

Paul: "Hmmm, not likely, those are the quick things to check. Have you checked any of the on-line discussion forums?"

> *Paul is with you on this project, not testing you for vulnerabilities. He's gathering data about your investigations.*

You: "Good idea. Thanks for not just throwing advice at me."

> *This stroke is very powerful in reinforcing his non-drama behavior. You're thanking him for not discounting you by means of advice.*

The underlying attitude here is that the two of you are equals. That helps to stop any discounting. Asking for what you want is obvious because it was done clearly - "You interested in working it through with me?"

In chapter three we talked about strokes and this final transaction is a good example of giving a stroke.

Sample 3: Flora is already home when Paul comes into the kitchen.

> *In this sample, the drama from Flora's point of view was called 'Kick Me'. And from Paul's point of view the drama was called 'See What You Made Me Do.' Except this time through I'll coach Flora on how to stay out of drama despite Paul's Victimhood.*

Paul: <*Flops down on the sofa with a groan*>

> *The groan is either a physiological or psychological expression of discomfort and not necessarily anything more. But, like the sigh in Sample 1 above, it could be an invitation for an inquiry from Flora, and if so is the first discount of self by not asking directly for what he wants – such as attention. If I was coaching Paul, I'd invite him to be clearer in his self-disclosures to inhibit others from jumping to conclusions.*

Flora: "Careful with that sofa. <*pause*> What's wrong?"

> *Flora first states her desire for care of the sofa. This is a simple statement of structure, no persecuting involved. Then she makes a request for information i.e. ask for what you want.*

Paul: "Nothin."

Flora: "Ah. Ok then."

> *Paul answers the question. Because he groaned in the first transaction, he has now contradicted himself. But it isn't Flora's job to point that out or follow up on it, as a therapist (who has a contract to do so) would. She asked a question, he answered it. She doesn't discount him this time; she simply accepts his response.*

Paul: "Is that all you gotta say, Ok then?"

> *If Paul was dedicated to pursuing the Victim position and since Flora is not in the drama, he could escalate the exchange at this point as another stronger invitation to her.*

Let's alter the original sample now with an attempt at escalation.

Flora: "No, I have more to say. I had a great time on the river this afternoon and I'd like to tell you about that. Will you listen?"

> *Flora responds to his query that she has nothing to talk about. But she does so without Persecuting. Instead she simply answers his question. Then she does some self-disclosure and asks for what she wants.*

Paul: "What? You wanna talk about fishing when I'm over here miserable?"

> *Paul discounts himself. That's the invitation to drama. He's miserable in some way that he is unwilling to articulate. He wants Flora to do the heavy digging – perform a rescue.*

Flora: "I'm listening if you want to tell me what's wrong."

> *Flora ignores the invitation to dig and again makes a simple statement. The ulterior transaction is something like 'You have the power to figure out what you want and then ask for it.'*

Paul: "Oh forget it Flora, just forget it." <gets up and walks out>

> *Paul takes his payoff as a Victim.*

To Flora's credit, she didn't discount Paul and see him as a Victim; she asked for what she wanted; she responded to his questions clearly. Concluding this set of transactions, Paul does the switch of positions even though Flora isn't in the drama with him.

Commonly the switch is to Persecutor with a comment like, "Oh forget it Flora, just forget it. And here I thought you cared about me. True colors showing now! What happened to the woman I married?"

What Flora needs to keep in mind front and center at this point is that Paul was steering for a dramatic conclusion like this right from the get-go. It proves some beliefs he has about himself, about women perhaps, about Flora, maybe about marriage.

Sample 4: While Flora finishes preparing dinner, stepfather Paul is setting the table. Teenage daughter Celina wanders in with iPod jacked headphones blaring a head banger. She leans against the counter facing step-dad.

> *The name we used for this drama from Celina's point of view was 'Let's You and Him Fight'. The first discount was, and still is from Celina with the loud music in a mutually shared*

physical space. This discount is her invitational stance as Persecutor. Flora and Paul each can decide to get involved in drama or not, the choices being as a Victim or as Persecutor (hoping to force Celina into Victim). In the original scenario, Flora got into Victim, Paul got into Rescuer of Flora; thus leaving Celina with her Persecutor role.

For our purpose, we'll change how Paul responds, leaving Flora to be Victim.

Flora: "Paul will you ask her to shut that noise off? It's giving me a headache."

Even though Flora is asking for what she wants, she opens the verbal sequence with two discounts. She first discounts her own ability to make a direct request of Celina. This is the setup for everything that follows; it's the bait. Another discount is her claim that the sound is creating a headache. If that was true both Paul and Celina would also be having headaches. No, the sound isn't responsible for Flora's headache.   Both these discounts put Flora on the Victim position.

Paul: "No I'm not willing to do that."

Paul has decided that doing for Flora what she could do for herself is a discount to her, and would constitute agreeing she was a Victim, thus making him a Rescuer. Nothing good comes from being a Rescuer – remember we're not talking about rescuers or real victims. So Paul states a clear no to Flora's request. This is an example of a boundary.

Flora: "What do you mean you're not willing to do that?"

Flora as Victim doesn't want a potential Rescuer to get away and spoil the potential drama; so she invites him again by discounting herself – she claims to be unable to understand what Paul's no means.

Paul: "I'm sure you can figure it out."

Here's another clear statement of a boundary, and a stroke: he's not willing to do her thinking for her because he's confident she can think for herself.

Flora: "Do I have to do everything around here?"

Notice how this isn't actually a question, it's a statement of one of Flora's beliefs, that she 'does everything around here'. Of course that's not true, so it's a quick Persecutory discount of Paul and Celina. Flora is still hoping to bait Paul into drama by

101

accusing him of not doing anything. He could respond defensively, she hopes, and attack her from Persecutor and then she would once again be in Victim. This two-step maneuver is common with Victims: jump to Persecutor for a slashing cut on the non-player, then back into Victim when the person gets into it with some defensive persecution of their own.

Paul: <silent>

Since Flora's question isn't a real question, he ignores it and keeps himself out of the drama that is clearly coming.

At this point in the sample, Celina will be unsatisfied in terms of her underlying unmet needs she was attempting to meet with drama. Flora will also be unsatisfied. So let's continue; but for instructional purposes, let's pretend Flora did a time-out for herself and read that last chapter.

Flora: <looking at Celina, makes a time-out gesture>

Celina: <nodding her head with the beat of the music, either doesn't see Flora, or pretends not to>

Could be a discount; but let's give Celina the benefit of the doubt.

Flora: <walks over right in front of Celina and waves her arms to get her attention, then makes the time-out hand sign>

Flora is problem solving her want with a request

Celina: <still nodding her head with the beat asks very loudly> "What?"

Celina executes a powerful discount of herself and Flora. Celina is pretending she doesn't understand the time-out hand sign, and that what Flora wants isn't important enough to do a time-out, or turn the volume down.

Flora: <looking at Celina, makes a time-out gesture>

Flora doesn't bite the bait of that discount. Instead she persists in her request for what she wants. In the background, she's developing a backup plan which we'll see below.

Celina: <rolls her eyes>

Another discount of Flora, this time of Flora's request.

Flora: *<gets two pots, positions herself in front of Celina and while looking her right in the eyes she bangs them together loudly>*

The backup plan. Creating a boundary that Celina has difficulty ignoring. This isn't a discount because nothing is being ignored. Flora is problem solving.

Celina: *<storms out of the room>*

Celina makes the switch from Persecutor to Victim, even though nobody is in the drama with her.

If a person really wants to get one of the dramatic payoffs I described in chapter three, the person cannot be stopped. And this ending shows how Celina did so. If she sat down with a therapist and did some introspective exploration, she might discover what her needs were; otherwise, she'll continue to use drama.

Sample 5 was Celina's solo drama; resolving it requires Celina to decide to refrain from discounting even in her day dream fantasy life. For many people, resolving fantasy drama is a low priority; after all, it's just a fantasy. But in fact, resolving day dream drama is of equal if not more importance than actual drama.

Here's why Celina might choose to change her discounting fantasies: what we practice becomes habit.

If we practice the Victim role, we're more likely to take on the Victim role – we get habituated as Victims.

If we practice the Rescuer role, we're more likely to take on the Rescuer role – we get habituated as Rescuers.

If we practice the Persecutor role, we're more likely to take on the Persecutor role – we get habituated as Persecutors.

The location of practice, in objective reality or fantasy land, makes no difference. Both practice sessions take place in the same mind. Celina's mind is practicing being Victim in the solo settings, the two person settings, and the three person settings. Even at a physiological level, neurologists confirm that repeated activation of a neural sequence sensitizes it to fire as a sequence. The phrase 'neurons that fire together wire together' applies to Celina repeatedly practicing a Victim role.

So what Celina must do is catch herself, be aware of herself, monitor her thoughts for discounts – and replace them with non-discounting thoughts such as appreciations.

Appreciations are antidotes to discounts.

Celina secludes herself in her bedroom. She's reviewing another 'look' her math teacher Ms. Davis gave her during class that afternoon. Using her diary, Celina writes the following:

Celina's Log, Stardate 15/4/2010 : 21:05 gmt

Ms. Davis looked at me again today, and I'm wondering what it meant. I could do a dramatic fantasy like last time; but Greg invited me to write a different kind of journal entry. Maybe I could ask her if the look meant anything about me instead of making up a meaning. A couple things I like about her: she's smart and clearly very capable in mathematics. And she does dress well for her age group. I'll ask her too, if she's marking me harder than the other girls. Being divorced must be a challenge. When I think about breaking up with my boyfriend I start to sweat, so breaking up her marriage had to be worse. I'm feeling some compassion for her situation; teaching math to a bunch of teens who don't want to learn. Teens can be harsh. I was harsh. She's probably a very nice person.

Celina is starting to change her attitude; taking a non-discounting stance.

Sample 6: After a quiet and tense dinner together with Flora, Celina gets up from the table and starts to leave the kitchen.

> *This is the version of drama called 'Wooden Leg'; where a participant uses a disability or infirmity, perceived or real, to get on the triangle as a Victim.*
>
> *The ability to listen for 'poor me' will help you in knowing if a person is into drama as Victim or not, regardless of real infirmities. A Victim will resist actually solving the real infirmity.*
>
> *In this revised sample, we'll have Flora stay out of drama but keep Celina in her Victim role (poor helpless Celina and her wired together neurons, it's her third time on the triangle in this chapter – even a fictional character can be a Victim, in this case of the mean writer Greg.)*

Flora: "Celina. Stop. Will you bring your dishes to the sink please?"

> *Clear directives. Clear requests. No discounting. Flora is standing in the attitude that Celina is a capable person.*

Celina: <puts on a 'pouty' face and returns to the table, then takes her dishes to the sink. She turns to leave the room>

> *Can you hear the 'poor me' violins playing in the background?*

Flora: "Celina, it's your turn to do the dishes. You willing to stick to your agreement?"

> *Flora gives a clear statement of a contract, and a request for fulfillment. Again Flora's attitude is that Celina is capable and powerful about her commitments.*

Celina: "Are you serious?"

Flora: <looks intently at Celina with silence>

> *Not really a question; it's a discount of herself being able to understand clear communication. Because it's not a real question, it's a request for a stroke disguised as a question about seriousness. Flora ignores it and hence doesn't reinforce Celina using these non-questions in future.*

Celina: "Aren't you forgetting I have an allergy to latex?"

> *Celina now discloses the discount to herself – she has a wooden leg (disability) and is therefore a Victim.*

Flora: "You willing to stick to your agreement?"

> *This goes to the heart of the matter with a question. Flora can do this because she sees Celina as a person who can know what she wants and ask questions, and make agreements.*

Celina: "Washing dishes – hot water – latex gloves - hives?"

> *Celina states the Victim position explicitly and ignores the question about her agreement. This is a discount of Flora.*

Flora: "Does that mean you're deciding to break our agreement?"

> *Flora requests clear confirmation that Celina has decided to cancel the agreement.*

Celina: "How can you expect someone with a latex allergy to just go ahead and expose themselves to it. Have you no sympathy?"

Celina ignores the question, reasserts her Victimhood and explicitly states that Flora is a Persecutor.

Flora: "I hear you Celina, you're breaking our contract. In that case, I'll decline to complete my part too."

Flora still isn't involved in the drama. She simply states the contract is null.

Celina: "What does that mean?"

Well dear reader, I decided Victim Celina should have some personal growth here in the book. So, she's asking a question in a clear manner.

Flora: "Is that a real question?"

Flora wants to know if Celina's question is another invitation to drama.

Celina: "I apologize for not remembering what we decided about kitchen responsibilities. Will you remind me?"

Oh my, she's off the Victim position for sure with that sincere apology and clear request for information. Way to go Celina! This opens the possibility of non-drama interactions.

Sample 7: Later that evening, as Flora is quietly reading, Celina approaches.

Celina: "Can I talk to you about something really important?"

Celina starts the set of transactions with a clear request?

Flora: <*Observing that Celina seems unusually quiet and polite, perhaps even sad, she sets her book down.*> "Sure honey, what's going on?"

Flora notices the body language and assumes something is going on with Celina. Using a term of endearment may be normal for Flora; but based on previous transactions we've witnessed with Paul and Celina, I doubt it. So Flora <u>may</u> be discounting by thinking something is wrong with Celina: poor helpless Celina.

Celina: <*Sits down beside Flora on the sofa, and starts to weep.*>

Celina could be simply sharing how she's feeling, or this could be a Victim inviting a Rescue.

Flora: <*Softly*>, "What is it? What's wrong?"

Flora rescues. The discount is that Flora doesn't wait for Celina to make a request, so the message from Flora is: 'There there poor dear, since you are incapable of activating yourself, I'll do it for you.' Notice that Flora does this softly, since tender little helpless Victims are so vulnerable. If Flora had the attitude that Celina was powerful enough to know what she wanted and ask for it, she wouldn't do Celina's task for her.

Celina: "Do you care about me?"

Celina asks a clear question. In fact it's a yes/no question. She's probably not in the Victim role. We suspect this because she's not conveying a 'poor me' message.

Flora: <*Feeling a sick twist in her stomach,*> "Of course I care about you. Why would you think such a thing?"

Flora started out attempting to Rescue, meaning she herself was emotionally on the triangle trying to get some dramatic exchange going with Celina as Victim. What do Victims do? They point at Persecutors. As such, Flora is feeling the fear of accusation as a Persecutor, even though Celina is not in the role of Victim.

Celina: "Well, <*starting to cry*> I'm imagining that my allergy means nothing to you compared to getting the dishes washed. Is that true?"

Celina has gone to the heart of the issue and asked for a reality check. She knows that her feelings come from her thoughts, and her thoughts could be fantasy. Notice the clear question.

Flora: <*Feeling relief*> "No. I am more concerned about your allergies than dishes."

Flora's decided not to stay in drama, she just answers the question.

Celina: "So <*drying her eyes*> my idea that you want me to move out in order to be alone with Paul, is that a boogey man story too?"

> *Celina decides to reality test another thought, with a clear question.*

Flora: <*Surprised.*> "Yes."

> *Flora answers the question.*

Celina: "Will you give me a hug?"

> *Celina asks for what she wants.*

Flora: "How bout we share a hug?"

> *Flora decides she wants a hug too; and asks for what will deliver hugs to both in a win-win.*

Although only three people took the roles in these samples, the same dynamics take place when multiple people take the roles.

Suppose two or more people get together on the Victim position, all singing 'poor us'. We could name the drama something like 'We are the Underdogs'. If the group got together in the Rescuer role we could name the drama something like 'Here We Come To Save the Day'. And if a group decided to be Persecutors they might call themselves 'Satan's Infidels'.

Take a look around your local society and guess what groups are in what roles.

In chapter four I mentioned how two or more people might joust for the role of Persecutor, with the loser moving to Victim. The same type of drama takes place when two or more people vie for sole occupation of the Victim position. Instead of overtly discounting the other (as two wanna-be Persecutors), two Victim prospects would compete in self-discounts as in 'I'm more of a loser than you are'. Each would claim some incompetence or infirmity or disability, and the other would out do it, or escalate it, or go-one-worse.

For example with two wanna-be victims V1 and V2 ...

Wanna-be V1: She'd never go out with me, I'm too short.

Wanna-be V2: That's not so bad. I wouldn't even show up on her radar, I'm too short and skinny.

Wanna-be V1: Yea but you've got character, I'm a door mat.

Wanna-be V2: No you're not. Talk about door mats, my middle name is Welcome.

Wanna-be V1: Ha. You've been rejected all of what, three times. I've been rejected, laughed at, stood up 13 times! Fired four times. Evicted twice. And divorced. I should get the Biggest Loser Award.

Wanna-be V2: But at least you got married and had sex. I've never even got past first base with a woman.

Wanna-be V1: You're still in the game at least. I've been kicked out of the stadium!

Wanna-be V2: All right all right, I concede. On another subject, sort of related, I bumped into your ex a few days ago actually. She asked me to go out sometime. Would you mind?

Wanna-be V1: I don't care. Go Ahead. She never asked me out.

In this sample, we also see the switch, when V2 concedes that V1 is the winner of the Victim position. V2 has to move to either Persecutor, Rescuer or Audience; and we see the move to Persecutor.

It's subtle but still an overt discount to say, 'I concede', and then begin talking about starting a relationship with V1's ex.

Chapter Summary

The major attitude change to stay drama free is this: you don't know how to author another person's life; and nobody else knows best how to author yours. The following behaviors manifest that idea:

- Stop discounting others.
- Listen for periods and question marks at the end of sentences. If it's not a question, don't answer one.
- Use active listening or data gathering questions instead of discounts.
- Establish contracts and boundaries, especially the word no.
- Ask for what you want.
- Don't join the debate society.

Mission Possible

Last time, pull out your personal drama sheet. What strategies will you use from the above list to stay drama free? Write them down. This is your plan to the drama free zone. I wish you good skill.

Chapter 6

Living in the Drama Free Zone

Won't Life Be Boring Without Drama?

I love conducting psychotherapy with young adults. If they're not depressed or anxious, young adults between the ages of 15 and 25 can be so zesty for life, that they can hardly contain themselves. When they self-disclose this exuberance to me, I smile inside and out.

I invited one such individual, a man, to be on my review board for this book. I was keen on having a young adult's perspective and energy, and he was willing to participate within the limitations of his academic and social needs and wants.

After reading chapter one and two, he emailed me some comments and then said he didn't want to be involved anymore. He explained that in his opinion most teens, himself included, <u>wanted</u> drama and would not read my book about how to stop it. *Life would be boring without it.*

The thing about a drama free life is that it's not dramatic; but that doesn't mean it has to be boring!

It is a choice to bore yourself!

Is this a boring sample?

Paul and Flora are 'relaxing' in front of the television watching the nightly news. *This time through, we'll watch the drama stop before it gets any momentum.*

Paul: "The world sure is going to hell."

> *Here's the first discount, ignoring positive aspects. It's actually what's called a cognitive distortion – overgeneralization. Doesn't sound like Paul's in the Rescuer role, so that leaves Victim or Persecutor.*

Flora: "Seems to me that these challenges offer opportunities for us to evolve as stewards of the planet."

> *Flora doesn't bite the invitation to get into drama. Instead she self-discloses.*

Paul: "Fat chance. We should just kiss our big butts goodbye."

> *But Paul isn't done. Here he reveals his inclination for Victim.*

Flora: "Let's find a program about positive action being taken; maybe get some ideas how we can participate. I hear concern and care from you. What do you say we switch channels?"

> *So Flora self-discloses what she wants, and makes an overt request. These are the key ingredients to prevent self-discounts and thus being a Victim – know what you want, asking questions to go in that direction. Notice how Flora strokes Paul for his concern.*

Paul: "Well it's not like I'm a radical tree hugger; but I do love the natural world and I hate to see its destruction. Yea, let's turn this off."

> *One of the motivations for drama is to get an exchange of strokes. When a person gets satisfied with strokes they exit drama. As such, Paul heard Flora's stroke and is now willing to move out of drama.*

Maybe I should subtitle this chapter ...

Nondramatic Anti-Boring Living

Boring is not a characteristic or attribute of anything in the real world. It's a personal decision as in, 'I <u>think</u> this chapter is boring.'

If boring was an attribute, like eye color, we'd all agree on it. Everybody who isn't color blind, who looks at my eyes will see what's called hazel colored eyes. But not everybody would agree they were boring.

Therefore, boring is a decision.

So, if you find yourself thinking that a nondramatic life will be boring, I invite you to re-decide that. It's a decision and not a fact.

And here's some strategies to use that will support you in that new decision.

Options And Strokes

Beware of a request for **constructive criticism** – it could be an invitation to drama. Instead, I hereby introduce you to **Options** and **Strokes** - a drama fighting dynamic duo to use when you are the listener invited to review or critically comment on someone's self-disclosure, idea, or creation[11]. I talked about strokes way back in chapter three and I'll give some examples below.

Options are alternative ideas and possibilities you are curious about, that relate to what the other person is asking for or disclosing. Options are not cold hard statements of facts, reality or truth.

Let's get right to an example, back to Sample 2.

Sample 2: You and your buddy Paul are sipping beers and watching the game Saturday afternoon. It's halftime and you casually start a conversation about your motor bike.

> *The sample will play out as before, with you not going into Victim nor inviting Paul to go into Rescuer. This time through, Paul will use the concept of options to participate.*

You: "Yea, I was out on the bike last night."

> *A straight forward self-disclosure.*

Paul: "Beauty of a night for it."

> *A clear self-disclosing statement of opinion.*

You: "Woulda bin, but the bike was running rough and I didn't get far."

> *Another self-disclosure.*

Paul: "How come?"

> *Clear easy honest question of curiosity.*

113

You: "Yea, good question. You interested in thinking it through with me?

> *A very powerful transaction this one, asking for collegial problem solving – as equals. No Victimhood here. An example of asking for what you want – contracting, that is founded on the attitude that you can know what you want and you can ask questions in order to figure out how to get what you want.*

Paul: "Sure. One option I can think of is dirty gas."

> *Here's the first option. An option is a simple self-disclosure of curiosity: a question as yet unanswered. There is no overt or covert discount.*

You: "I just filled up, and replaced both the gas and air filters, and the plugs a week ago. Do you think it could be dirty gas even so?"

> *You're participating in the inquiry by supplying factual data.*

Paul: "Hmmm, not likely, I think you've covered the quick things to check. I'm wondering what the online discussion forums might have to say?"

> *Paul strokes you with the 'you've covered the quick things to check', and the option is expressed clearly as a curiosity.*

You: "Good idea. Thanks for not just throwing advice at me."

> *Here, you stroke Paul for the drama free interchange.*

Many meetings degenerate into drama with the misuse of 'constructive criticism'. Many people make statements of facts and data as truths, thinking it's helpful; but the potential for discounting is high when doing so.

Have you ever heard this post-drama lament, "I just told the truth/facts. Why did she/he take it the wrong way?" The reason for drama when reciting facts is that by stating facts and truths you could be sending this discounting message, 'Because I state factual data and you did not, it means I know more than you. I'm smarter than you. Take a seat here at my feet with your notebook little one, and I will tell you how it is.'

Here's a few ways to deliver options instead:

- An option I'm wondering about is <*fill in the blank*>.

- Something I've had success with that I'm thinking might work here is <*fill in the blank*>.
- I've heard about people who, in this situation, had success using <*fill in the blank*>.
- As you were talking I was pondering what might happen if <*fill in the blank*>.
- Do you think there's any chance <*fill in the blank*> will work?
- I'm imagining this down the line, and wondering if <*fill in the blank*> could happen.
- I wonder what the big deal experts would say about this. Any info on that?
- I had a similar experience and I remember afterwards thinking, *What about <fill in the blank>*? So I'm back to that question for you, what about <*fill in the blank*>?
- I'm thinking about consequences, and wondering, *If <fill in the blank> then what are the odds <fill in the blank> will happen*?

The stroking component can precede or follow the option. And like an option it's a self-disclosure, not a claim of the other person's omnipotence. When a stroke includes evidence, it is very powerful since the person cannot discount it. Wanna-be Victims have a hard time denying anti-discount proof.

- I like the way you said <*specific statement*>.
- The point you made about <*specific idea*> I found very interesting and tells me you have insight.
- Your concern about <*specifically what the concern was*> tells me you are thoughtful about <*the subject*> and I appreciate that.
- In my opinion, you demonstrate excellence in <*specific attribute*> when you <*specific behavior*>.
- I read about <*whatever the subject is*> and you used the same successful strategy. Nice.
- I appreciate how you <*specifically noteworthy behavior*>
- When you <*specific behavior*> I decided you were showing <*a quality*>.
- I like how you approached this, your method was sound, even with data that in hindsight was skewed.
- I like the energy you put into this; shows your commitment.

Another method of staying drama free but having an interesting life is to …

Look For Opportunities Inside Challenges

Maybe the slogan, 'there's a silver lining in every cloud', has been overdone, and maybe you've heard it a thousand times. Maybe you'll challenge yourself with boredom in the next few paragraphs.

If so, one possible option I'm thinking I'd consider if I was a reader is to relax and enjoy the read as a review. That is itself looking for opportunities inside challenges! Notice too that just now I didn't discount you with advice; I offered an option I was thinking of.

Finding opportunities inside challenges is anything but boring in my opinion.

For me, snooping around, poking my inquisitive nose into corners and cracks of a situation is interesting. I say to my young adult clients that it's their particular developmental task to stick their fingers into the sockets of life and feel for electricity; find out what 'turns their crank' and 'floats their boat'; discover where the juice is; where the fire is; how much of a zap can they accept.

Joseph Campbell has said, 'follow your bliss', and what he meant by that was to taste test life and find out what is sweet and what is sour. Then track the sweet. That's the essence of exploring a challenge for opportunities.

This isn't a mind game, trying to 'talk yourself' into liking or tolerating something.

This is truth seeking - <u>your truth</u> about how expansive you are.

Can you expand into challenges?

Can you fill the space of your human life?

Can you experience all of being human?

Explore and Test Your Reality for Validity

In chapter four I introduced *active listening* as a method of establishing boundaries, and understanding someone else's (the self-discloser's) reality. Here I introduce another interpersonal skill, a method of clarifying your reality – to see if it's valid.

Sample: My wife Barbara and I are on a date night, and out dancing. During a slow foxtrot she turns her face toward me and looks at me with a facial expression. (This really did happen; several times. Fortunately for our marriage we're both skilled in checking out our realities with each other.)

Here's what happened next.

Greg: "What?"

> *Well, most of us have old programming that slips past and that's what this is. This is a feeble way of asking what I've done wrong. Can you sniff my Victim stance?*

Barbara: "What what?"

> *She playfully asks what I'm asking about.*

Greg: "I'm seeing you look at me and I'm thinking you don't like the way I'm dancing. Is that true?"

> *So now I get myself connected to my skillfulness, out of Victim, and ask the underlying question. I'm checking my reality for validity.*

Barbara: "No. I'm loving this."

> *Well what-da-ya-know, my version of reality is incorrect.*

Many misunderstandings take place between people because huge assumptions of reality occur without any validity checking.

In this sample, I was thinking she was angry or sad about my dancing. If I had not tested that assumption, thinking instead it was true reality, I might have quit and walked off the dance floor. Worse, I might have gone into a pout or sulk and maybe given her the 'silent treatment'. She might have reacted with her own erroneous assumption and the evening could have careened into drama very easily.

Instead, I tested reality by asking her to confirm my version. She self-disclosed her reality; and I updated mine with better data.

If you're a novice at this, and want to add it to your skill set, here's what is called an **interpersonal communication structure**.

As you become skilled at using it, you can shorten it to suit the situation, like I did in the sample. There's a more advanced version coming along below.

Here's what you say to the other person in order to check into your version of reality: "When I hear you say or do <something observable> I think <whatever it is>. Is that true?"

Examples concerning your assumptions about another person:

- When you say you don't care where we go out to eat, I'm thinking you'd rather not dine out. Is that true?

- When I ask you if you're mad at me and you shout No. I'm thinking you sure sound angry. Is it really true you're not angry at me?

- When I ask you a question and you don't answer, I'm thinking there is an issue between us. Is that true?

- When you are silent for more than an hour, I'm thinking you're upset with me. Is that true?

- When I see your face change into tight and drawn, as it is now, I'm thinking you're experiencing some big feelings. Is that true?

- When you say you don't care what I get you for a birthday gift, I'm thinking you don't want me to care about you. Is that true?

- When I see you look at that woman's backside I'm thinking you want to have sex with her. Is that true?

- When I see you talking with him so closely I'm thinking you're not happy with me and want to split up. Is that true?

- When I said that thing about your mother, I saw you grimace. I'm thinking you're insulted. Is that true?

I invite you to delve into your version like an underwater explorer. Poke around and find out what fantasies you've got going on.

This investigation into your reality will reveal all sorts of unreal ideas and beliefs. For many of them, they were real at one time; but they

118

apply only rarely or never at all anymore. If you do not challenge them, you will live in a non-real world continuously either perplexed about what you and others are thinking, feeling, and doing; or assume you know and respond ineffectively or inappropriately.

I invite you to make that investigation interesting and perhaps exciting.

Want more excitement? Add this next skill.

Advanced Self Exploration and Reality Checking

Going to the next level now...

This is an interpersonal skill for those of you who enjoy the taste of personal power and effectiveness dealing with others. It builds on that last communication structure. In this version, you add what you're feeling, and what the meaning is. Here's the general structure:

"When I hear you say or do *<something observable>*, I feel *<what I'm feeling – i.e. happy sad angry excited or afraid>*, because I'm thinking *<what my thoughts are>*. I'm responsible for making this mean *<what the meaning of the thoughts are>*. Do you think that meaning is true?"

Examples:

- When you say you don't care where we go out to eat, I feel sad because I'm thinking you'd rather not dine out. I'm responsible for making this mean you actually don't want to go out to dinner with me. Do you think that meaning is true?

- When I ask you if you're mad at me and you shout No, I feel scared because I'm thinking you sure sound angry. I'm responsible for making this mean I don't understand why you shout if you're not mad at me. Do you think you're not angry at me when you shout?

- When I ask you a question and you don't answer, I feel scared because I'm thinking there is an issue between us. I'm responsible for making it mean we're in trouble. Do you think that meaning true?

119

- When you are silent for more than an hour, I feel angry because I'm thinking you're upset with me. I'm responsible for making that mean you want to punish me with a silent treatment. Do you think that meaning is true?

- When I see your face change into tight and drawn, as it is now, I feel anxious because I'm thinking you're experiencing some big feelings. I'm responsible for making that mean something is very wrong. Do you think that's true?

- When you say you don't care what I get you for a birthday gift, I feel sad because I'm thinking you don't want me to care about you. I'm responsible for making that mean you want to break up with me. Do you think that meaning is true?

- When I see you look at that woman's backside I feel jealous because I'm thinking you want to have sex with her. I'm responsible for making this mean you're not happy with our sex life. Do you think that meaning is true?

- When I see you talking with him so closely I feel angry because I'm thinking you're not happy with me and want to split up. I'm responsible for making that mean I'm not good enough for you. Do you think that meaning is true?

- When I said that thing about your mother, I saw you grimace. I feel guilty because I'm thinking you're insulted. I'm responsible for making that mean I shouldn't have been so blunt. Is that true?

The cool part of this structure is that you get to find out how you create your own reality; and how it is different from other people's reality. I'm not talking about hard physical reality. I'm talking about the soft inner version where meaning-making takes place. It is in that space that drama takes place. It's also in that space that intimacy takes place. In fact, it's in that space where all interpersonal interactions take place.

The better you know how you create yours, the better you can respect and understand the inner reality that others create and live in. For me, there is nothing boring about that.

For example: I was at a six day residential training event a while ago. About three days in, at lunch in the dining hall, three of us were sitting together and chatting when another participant joined us. Let's call him Bob and the other three therapists T1, T2 and T3. When there was a natural break in our conversation, Bob started a new topic.

Bob: "I really don't see why we need to learn this new method when the proven one worked so well. This is such a waste of time and money."

T1:   "Why'd you come?"

Bob: "I was seduced by the advertising. I was perfectly happy and effective; now I'm so mixed up. This new material is such a joke."

T2:   "I see it being quite helpful actually."

Bob: "Well you must have a very different client population than me. I have to use standard CBT to keep my referrals coming from doctors. I'm at their whim."

T3:   "My referring physicians don't care what I use, as long as I give a good service."

Bob: "What planet do you live on? I should move there."

At this point I was finished eating and wanted to resign from the audience so I got up and took my dishes to the dishwashing station. A few minutes later on my way out of the dining hall, I could see the drama was continuing back at the table. I'll continue this story in a moment but something worth pointing out is how Bob flitted between Victim and Persecutor very quickly. He wasn't waiting for a switch.

Bob was walking down the hall towards me about 20 minutes later. I was leaning against the wall reading a brochure.

Bob: *<with energy>* "I just gotta say something to you."

Greg: "Ok I have five minutes to listen."

Bob: "Is it me or what? I mean I sat down for lunch and within six minutes everyone at the table gets up and leaves. I was just stating my opinion, and apparently it's the wrong opinion, or I'm crazy, or nobody's supposed to think critically. Like my damned family, never any time for me. I'm really angry."

121

Greg: "Are you angry with me, is that what you're saying?"

Bob: "No, no, not you. I feel safe telling you that's all."

Greg: "Ok, I've still got three minutes. What would you like from me?"

Bob: "I think I just needed to get that off my chest. <sigh> Do you like this new method?"

Greg: "I like adding options to my tool box. So yes I do."

This interchange between Bob and I was not drama; and it wasn't boring. He started in Victim but left the position when I didn't participate. I set clear time boundaries, asked a yes/no question, asked what he wanted from me, and answered his clearly stated question. The reason he felt safe with me was because he'd already observed and experienced me staying out of drama for three days of intense interpersonal and personal growth work.

Chapter Summary

Being bored is a choice. Having a boring life is a choice. Being free of drama does not result in boredom. A non-boring life can be created with strategies that also help keep you out of drama: options and strokes, looking for opportunities inside challenges, reality testing, exploring self and reality.

Mission Possible

I invite you to pay attention to all situations where you observe or experience Victims, Rescuers, or Persecutors. The daily news is an excellent resource for this practice. Drama can range from solo to international in scope, conducted at all three levels of intensity (from chapter two).

Another little suggestion here, listen to pop song lyrics and you'll hear a lot of stories about drama.

Chapter 7

A Dramatic Finish?

Your Choice!

Taking Personal Responsibility

With this book my contract with you was...

> to describe a pervasive pattern of interpersonal relations, called drama; to describe it in such a way that you could identify it when you experience it or see it; to exit from it and/or refuse to get into it; to engage in other ways of interacting with people.

Your part of the contract was to be receptive and open to new ideas. I hope you've kept your side of the agreement. If so, consider that you've taken responsibility for your life.

I've pondered many hours how I should write these closing words. The standard and safely acceptable method would be to summarize. I'm thinking no, I want instead, to step into who I am becoming even more visibly than what I've written so far.

I invite you to do likewise; to launch what you've read up to now. So for me, here's the final most compelling point of **No More Drama**.

I've had the privilege of sitting beside and being with five dying family members. Many of you have probably had the honor as well. Three of them chose to relax, review the highlights of their life, and say their goodbyes with love. The other two chose bitterness and resentment, resisting and protesting the 'wrongness' of this outcome.

Victims. That's how they authored their last days and that's how I remember them. That's their legacy.

*How do **you** want to live in your final days as a human? What legacy do you want to leave?*

I ask you this because each day is a practice for that time. If you practice drama, you will have drama as the curtain falls. Drama will be your legacy. If you practice a drama free life, your final moments will probably be in peace and love, and that will be your legacy.

Many people dodge this question of how to live in the final days.

They say they don't want to think about the inevitable, that it's a sad subject or a depressing topic. Some people will distract themselves from their appointment with eternity using substances or activities. Some people create heroic fantasies instead of facing a realistic scene.

Will these folks have the consciousness of personal responsibility to approach the moment with grace? The probability is low.

On the other hand, if you dear reader, take 100% responsibility for how you live each moment, you will be skillful, knowledgeable, and practiced in living every breath up to your last.

Mission Possible

Your life is ahead. I invite you to author it with joy instead of drama.

Chapter Summary

People who want milk should not seat themselves in the middle of a field with stool and bucket and wait for a dairy cow to back up to them.

The Sun Never Says

Even after all this time, the sun never says to the earth "You owe me."

Look what happens with a love like that. It lights the Whole Sky.

- Hafiz

Endnotes

1) All the sample names originate with a book written by Dr. Eric Berne, the founder of Transactional Analysis (TA), titled *Games People Play*, published in 1964.
Dr. Berne promoted the idea that TA should use common every-day language. That was my intention as well. Hence what I've called drama in this text is actually referred to as a psychological game in TA. Readers interested in psychological games could start further inquiry with the book *TA Today* by Ian Stewart and Vann Joines.

2) The term Mission Possible is one I first heard from my TA mentor Clark Reed in the late 1980s. Some psychotherapists use the word 'homework' to describe client activity between therapy sessions. I prefer mission possible because I think it lowers the probability that a client will put me in a one-up position, or if so, not so high up.

3) Contracting is a vitally important component of TA theory and practice. Contracting has its philosophical roots in the TA stance that people are ok; meaning that neither the client nor the therapist are one-up or one-down – that both are capable of thoughts, feelings, behaviors, and changing any or all of these.
From this stance, contracts facilitate the therapy process by dividing responsibilities into the client's 'what' to change and the therapist's "how" to invite the change. Contracts invite both client and therapist to be realistic in that the outcomes must be observable, verifiable or experientially measurable.
A contract guards against imposing or pursuing covert agendas or the therapist's idea of treatment outcomes on the client.
In essence, a contract is a plan for arrival at a desired destination. A great number of TA people have contributed to the 'state of the art' of contracting in relationships.

4) Discounts, discounting, and passivity were brought into TA theory and practice between 1971 and 1975 by Aaron and Jaqui Schiff.

5) The original set of transactions was called a *Psychological Game*, and Berne devised an ingenious system of analysis that he presents in Games People Play. He later modified his

system into what is called Formula G, which included what's called the gimmick and the switch.

Stephen Karpman noticed that many psychological games included the three dramatic roles so familiar in fairy tales. Readers interested in Karpman's development of the Drama Triangle could visit his website (2011): www.KarpmanDramaTriangle.com.

Alberto Villoldo refers to The Triangle of Disempowerment in his book *The Four Insights*. This version, as he describes it, sounds similar if not the same as what we're discussing here.

6) Degrees of intensity of a psychological game was an idea Eric Berne came up with. I've wondered if he used degrees of burns as a synonym or as a metaphor of his surname.

7) Claude Steiner came up with the idea of a stroke economy and published it in 1971.

8) Technically speaking from a TA theory point of view, the word drama isn't used. Psychological game is the second most intense exchange of strokes in the time structural continuum.

9) Forgiveness is a huge topic in psychology and psychotherapy, and perhaps an even greater topic in religious studies; and from my readings of this material, getting out of drama is **fundamental** to each understanding.

10) Grade school children were asked, "How do you get what you want from your parents?' They responded by saying they keep asking. Researchers asked, "How many times do you ask?" The national average was nine times. One boy had conducted his own study and discovered he was granted an Xbox after 56 requests! When I heard this research finding I was years away from writing this book so I don't have a citation for the study. If you know it, I'd be grateful if you'd email it to me (go to www.NoMoreDrama.ca for an email address).

11) Options and Strokes is an operation I learned from one of my mentors, Vann Joines, as a component of psychotherapy supervision. For those readers who are therapists or healers using supervision as a tool of oversight and skill development, I highly recommend options and strokes. It facilitates learning and minimizes discomfort. Imagine presenting a case in group supervision where the feedback was options and strokes: "An option was to confront the client's narcissism, hopefully to reveal the underlying wound. I liked the way you invited her to experience her feelings about the ..."

Index

CPSIA information can be obtained
at www.ICGtesting.com
Printed in the USA
LVOW03s0824241117
557348LV00004B/389/P